The Captured Ones

From Jim Bradshaw, Grand Forks
7/21/14

The Captured Ones

✦

American Prisoners of War in Germany
1944-1945

Erik Dyreborg

iUniverse, Inc.
New York Lincoln Shanghai

The Captured Ones
American Prisoners of War in Germany 1944-1945

Copyright © 2006 by Erik Dyreborg

All rights reserved. No part of this book may be used or reproduced by any means, graphic, electronic, or mechanical, including photocopying, recording, taping or by any information storage retrieval system without the written permission of the publisher except in the case of brief quotations embodied in critical articles and reviews.

iUniverse books may be ordered through booksellers or by contacting:

iUniverse
2021 Pine Lake Road, Suite 100
Lincoln, NE 68512
www.iuniverse.com
1-800-Authors (1-800-288-4677)

ISBN-13: 978-0-595-39781-5 (pbk)
ISBN-13: 978-0-595-84188-2 (ebk)
ISBN-10: 0-595-39781-6 (pbk)
ISBN-10: 0-595-84188-0 (ebk)

Printed in the United States of America

Contents

Foreword..................................... vii

Lyle's List.................................... *1*

The Experience............................. *19*

The 9/11................................... *151*

Selected Pictures.......................... *181*

Afterword....................................189

Foreword

by Steven Lian

My father, Elmer T. Lian, was an airman during World War II. His aircraft was shot down over Europe and he had been held prisoner in a German Prisoner of War Camp for over seven months.

As a youngster in the early 1950s, I recall playing with some of the items my Dad had made while in that prison camp. I didn't know much about POWs and certainly less about war, but I did know that these were special items and represented something that had happened in my Dad's life. Among these items was a cigarette package case made of woven metal strips from KLIM (powdered milk) cans, a cigarette lighter made from a shell casing, and several notebooks with covers made from flattened KLIM cans and held together by wire and string. I had no idea of the significance of these items or what the notebooks held until I grew up.

During my youth, I also heard stories of flying B-24s and B-17s, men parachuting out of crippled planes, my Dad watching planes go down next to his and wondering if he would be the next to fall.

This book contains stories of young Americans who were "just doing their jobs" but who were, in reality, dying for their country. The lucky ones came home alive. Death was always just around the corner, yet they mustered the courage to go out each day and do what they'd been sent to do. These stories represent but a fraction of the WWII's generation's dedication to wiping out a ruthless empire. They fought so America could stay free and to free other countries who believed freedom should be a way of life.

I also remember that as a child, we always had a large freezer full of food including frozen items such as watermelon and milk to make sure we never ran out of food. You will learn from the stories in this book the reasons an ex POW might do this. No one comes back from war the same as he or she went in. In all wars, including the present war in Iraq, there is a group of soldiers who have wounds that are not visible. We can better understand these hidden wounds when we learn the stories of these people.

Like many things in life, we do not appreciate events in another's life until we have matured. I had read the materials my father put together over the years, but the meaning of these events did not hit home until I attended one of the survivors reunions with my father in 2000 at Jackson Hole, Wyoming.

My father did what he had been doing for years—recording the recollections of WWII airpower veterans. He felt it was very important to document the ways these men survived and to pass this information on future generations. Dad said to me many times, "You know, we (WWII veterans) are dying off by the thousands each year and pretty soon there won't be anyone left to tell our stories."

My father died June 2, 2001, but his story and the stories of others like him will be passed on due to the efforts of authors like Erik Dyreborg. Erik realizes the importance of documenting events for future generations; he appreciates the veterans stories as will you, when you read his books.

I am grateful to Erik for taking on this project and adding to our knowledge of WWII airmen. My father would be extremely pleased with Erik's books and honored that his story is included in one of them.

Lyle's List

Introduction by Lyle Shafer, B-17 pilot

8th Air Force, 390th Bomb Group, 569th Bomb Squadron

Edited by Erik Dyreborg

Lyle Shafer, 1944 is pictured above

An air of anticipation hung heavily over the camp. For two or three weeks there was a systematic series of explosions in the area. We at first believed it might be the approaching Russian army. Then we realized that it was a form of scorched earth policy being carried out by the Germans. We had been digging fox holes and trenches in the event the camp was shelled or bombed inasmuch as we were in the path of the allies from the west and the Russians from the east. We were also led to believe that we might be marched out ahead of the advancing Russian troops. In any event, liberation seemed imminent.

We were eager to go home. The routine of our lives had been shattered and we had some fear we may not escape the end of the war without further harm. The feeling that prevailed throughout the camp was one of uncertainty, the same uncertainty that pervaded the camp during our stay. There was no solid rock upon which to rely. The camp's German military, the Allied internal camp hierarchy and in fact the individual prisoners provided little or no feeling of comfort. Each man felt himself an equal to each of the other prisoners, and perhaps because of that, acted alone and felt alone.

Most of the men in the camp followed the same basic pattern. It was almost like building an individual cocoon to protect themselves. Each kept his own counsel and awaited his time to get back to a normal life. It was not a period of socializing. After nine months, of the over 9,000 prisoners in the camp, I only knew a few other than the men in my room, and one of those was the navigator who was shot down with me.

As part of a bomber crew, along with nine other men, I was assigned to a B-17 for training in preparation for shipment to a combat unit. We all became good friends through the experience and flew 25 missions before being shot down over the target at Nuremburg, Germany. The crew was a family. After I miraculously escaped the exploding bomber, I landed in an open patch of land in the suburb of Schweinau. I thought I was the only one of the ten man crew to survive. I learned later that my navigator, Duward Bare, had been blown from the exploding plane and my tail gunner, Ben Howell, had crawled out of the severed tail. All three survivors were injured. I made a number of promises to myself, none of which I kept. One of them was, "do not develop close friendships with fellow soldiers. It is too traumatic when you lose them". I felt that way during the early days of my stay at the prisoner of war camp. However, before the war ended, and ever since, I learned that knowing, making and appreciating friends, would far outweigh the sadness felt if I ever lost them. I suspect each of the roommates went through the same thought process.

I found, the longer I stayed in the room where my roommates and I were housed, the more I recognized how much I would be missing them, if I did not keep in touch with them after we each went our separate ways. I was not certain they felt the same way, but I proceeded to ask each of them for their home address with the admonishment that after the war I would try to find them. The list I compiled was of 23 roommates and the 2 prisoners who served as the barracks officers in the small two person room next to ours. The addresses were given to me with a great amount of skepticism, but given nevertheless. Most of the addresses were limited to the home of their respective parents and consisted of the roommate's name or nickname and the town or city of his parents. I stuffed the list in my pocket and thought little more about it for several years, although I always kept the list.

Like most all of the veterans of WW II, other than those who elected to pursue a military career, we all returned home and attempted to pick up where our lives had been detoured three years previously. Most went to college, or started businesses or pursued a wide range of activities.

My employment required me to move around the country from time to time and I always tried to find a roommate or two. I was seldom successful. However, commencing about 1972, I started a thorough search in earnest for the roommates. The search extended over 17 years.

Lyle's List

The above is a copy of the original list, covering all the roommates. The list was made by Lyle Shafer, during his stay in Stalag Luft I, Barth, Germany from 1944 to 1945.

About the roommates

As individuals, the roommates were about as diverse a group as one could imagine. All were in their twenties, with most only 20, 21 or 22. Very few were married. However, the longer we were together, instead of falling apart into small cliques, we grew into one unit. Bonding grew day by day and became strong. We came out of our cocoons (not butterflies, unfortunately) but seasoned veterans despite our tender ages.

The food was distributed to individuals in each room. Pressed bricks of coal were distributed to the rooms. The food was consolidated by the roommates into what was referred to throughout the camp as a "combine". The food was cooked in the room for the "combine" and the group ate each of their two "meals" together. It has always been my belief that sitting down to a meal together fortified the bonding that had been taking place. It didn't matter that there was little to eat, it was the process that was important.

Bread was thinly sliced and each man was given his share. Our bread slicer, "Whitey Schlueter" did a superb job and was never replaced. Turns were taken doing the cooking and washing the dishes. The makeup of combines was a source of great arguments and complaining. As a result, some rooms would have as many as four or five separate combines. This grew worse as the food shortage increased. Some combines consisted of only one or two men. However, our combine never split into smaller units. We stayed as one combine. This was typical of the way the roommates lived. There was much give and take, of course, on most all subjects imaginable, but we stayed as one unit. That increasingly impressed me as I grew to realize that this group of roommates was unique.

I was successful in finding all but three of the roommates. Three had died but I found the three families. I corresponded with each of the roommates and when possible visited them during my trips around the country. Finding them was not easy, however, because this was prior to the internet and they were scattered throughout the United States.

It is a privilege to introduce you to an outstanding group of men: who during a time of great need, answered the call to serve their country in the military; who survived that assignment under trying circumstances; and who returned home to contribute in a substantial way to the society in which we live.

Finding the roommates
Rolland Olson, Pilot
Howard Ray, Pilot
Robert drew, Pilot

The easiest one to find was Rolland Olson. He had given me his address as Zumbrota, Minnesota. It was Oley Olson, from Zumbrota, Minnesota. I never forgot that one. It had a great rhythm. I contacted the Zumbrota post office and talked to the manager. He knew exactly how I could reach Oley who was living in Chicago. When I quizzed Oley about how the postmaster knew his whereabouts, Oley explained that they had been high school classmates and knew one another and each other's family who lived in the Zumbrota area. Oley's mother and father lived on a nearby farm.

Two of Oley's crew who survived the "shoot down" were roommates: Bob Drew, bombardier and Howard Ray, navigator. He knew their whereabouts and I located them with ease. Oley owned and operated a Plymouth car agency in Chicago following the end of the war and later worked for the U.S. Government in its contracts operation. Ray was the marketing manager with USS Agri Chemicals located in Atlanta GA. Bob Drew was the owner and operator of a large dairy farm located at Rice Lake WI.

Oran Fulton, Bombardier
Robert McFall, Bombardier
J. William Haney, Navigator

My business duties sometimes required me to be in the Los Angeles area. I knew Oran Fulton had joined the L.A. police force and felt that was the best place for me to start. I marched into the main police station at a time the policemen were changing shifts and was told to try the shower room. They thought Oran was there. He wasn't. It seemed like there were hundreds of other guys roaming around, laughing, talking to one another, hustling to take showers, snapping each other on their naked bodies with a wet towel, dress into their off duty clothing and head for home—but there was no Oran. He was in the field on duty.

At a later date, I was able to catch Oran at the police station and talk with him. I asked him about Robert "Red" McFall who had given me an L.A. address. Oran gave me a couple of suggestions that paid off and I located and met with "Red". Red worked in marketing for a pharmaceutical firm and was later engaged in house building and real estate. In talking to the two of them I was told that Bill Haney had moved to Tucson from L.A. It was a fairly simple matter to locate Bill. He had his own CPA firm in Tucson and was listed in the telephone book.

As it turned out, Robert McFall had, prior to my meeting with Oran, contacted Oran and ask Oran to vouch for him inasmuch as Red had been given a speeding ticket. Oran was a straight up and down kind of guy and told Red to "take a hike". Like the Texas saying "don't mess with Texas"; with Oran it was always "don't mess with Fulton".

Lauren Schwisow, Pilot

Oran was a crew member of Lauren Schwisow, another roommate, and he gave me enough clues to enable me to find Lauren. Lauren and his wife Reta, school mates and married prior to Lauren going over seas, lived in Nebraska. Lauren later became a school teacher, coach and administrator, finishing his career in a suburb of Chicago as a school superintendent. It was not difficult finding Lauren with Oran's help.

Howard "Bud" Brown, Navigator

Another original resident of Nebraska, Howard "Bud" Brown, lived in Omaha. I had little information to help me in finding Bud and the search took a couple of years. I found that he worked for a meat packing company in Omaha prior to the service in the army, but the company provided no valid clues to follow. I originally tried the usual approach by trying to reach the Omaha address he had given me first by telephone and then by writing. The letter was returned, stating "no house at this address".

I used another standard approach of checking public records, including the high school where I believed there was a chance Brown had attended. I asked a friend of mine in Omaha to send an associate to the school to check it out. He was referred to the head of a class reunion group. He was informed that a Howard Brown had attended that particular high school and class; that he was in combat in Europe; that he was a POW; but was now deceased. However, he provided the name and city of his mother who at that time was living in Iowa. I eventually found the mother and she confirmed that her son, Howard Brown, was indeed a prisoner of war in Germany. I quizzed her about his military position in the army and was told he was in the infantry. In contrast to the Howard Brown I was searching for, her son was about 6' 6" while my roommate was about 5' 6". It was a disappointment to say the least.

Sometime later, after searching military records, retired military associations and similar civilian records, I returned to the beginning I used to start all my searches. I wrote another letter to the address he had given me in 1945. Only this time I addressed the letter to "Occupant". Before long I received a letter from the man who lived next door. The postman had delivered this letter addressed to "occupant" to him. He told me when Howard's parents moved, he had purchased the house and had it razed to provide more land space for his house. He knew Howard and gave me his current address. Howard had followed a career in the Air Force; was retired; and he and his wife lived at Sun City, Arizona. That was only a 45 minute drive from my winter home in Scottsdale, Arizona. I immediately arranged a meeting. As you can no doubt imagine, trying to locate a man named "Brown" in the U. S. was not an easy task.

Willis T. Jones, Jr., Bombardier

Captain Willis T. Jones, Jr., the internal military administrative officer who roomed in the 2 man room next to ours with Captain Carmen "Dusty" Rhoades, the barracks commander, had given me the simple address W.T. Jones, Goosecreek, Texas. I tried the telephone system first and was told they had no listings for Goosecreek, Texas. I wrote a letter to W.T. Jones at Goosecreek, Texas and was told by the postal authorities there was no such town in Texas. I found it difficult to accept that Jones had given me a phony name. By and by, when other attempts to locate him failed, in November, 1973, I wrote a letter to "Postmaster, Goosecreek, Texas" and explained my dilemma. Later, I received the required information from M. L. Neal, Postmaster, Baytown, stating: that Texas at one time had a town by the name of Goosecreek; that it was merged into Baytown, Texas following the end of WW II; that the school district remained Goosecreek School District; that my friend was a physician who at that time was serving as the Chief of Anesthesiology at Gulf Coast Hospital in Baytown.; and that he had contacted my friend who was now waiting to hear from me.

Robert Pearce, Bombardier

After the normal search was made through the telephone and letter writing, I always contacted the Chamber of Commerce of the town where I was trying to locate a roommate. Often so much time had elapsed they had little information that could help me. However, sometimes it paid off. Robert Pearce was one of them. His folks lived in Birmingham AL and I tried the chamber of commerce when my regular searches failed. I got Bob's name from the Birmingham Chamber of Commerce. Bob had pursued a career in the Air Force but had returned to his home base. At the time I found him, he had retired from the marketing organization of a Birmingham Steel company.

Jack Wierman, Pilot

The Chamber of Commerce for the Harrisburg PA area gave me the address for two men named John Wierman. I hit pay dirt on the second try. John had been a builder of houses in the area. I talked with him on the telephone and found that he had been trying for years to find some of his roommates, to no avail. John was very ill when I found him and he died a few weeks later, never able to visit with any of his roommates.

Joe Bingham, Pilot

It was interesting to me to learn of all the roommates who left their home town, worked a career in another town or State only to return home to the family nest after retirement. Joe Bingham was a case in point. He gave me his address as Rochester, New York. By the time I tried to reach him there were no Binghams listed in the telephone directory. Joe, after graduating from law school, became a CPA and spent his working career in Florida. He never married. I continued to search for him to no avail. Several years later, I started my search for Joe from the beginning. I tried the telephone service again. The results were the same. No Binghams listed. And the telephone operator could find no Binghams with unlisted numbers. Remembering some assistance I had earlier received in a search for another person, I asked the local Chamber of Commerce if they would give me the names of all Binghams listed in Rochester plus all the Binghams listed in the Rochester suburbs and general area. Again there were no Binghams in Rochester but there were a couple of Binghams in a suburb. Luckily, the first Bingham I called was Joe's brother. Joe had just recently retired and left Florida to return to the Rochester area and his family. I explained the reason for my call and Joe's brother replied "Joe just returned to the Rochester area and lives next door".

Elmer T. Lian, Pilot

Elmer was a career officer of the Air Force and when he retired he moved back to his home town of Grand Forks ND. He was another person who had returned to his home town after a career that took him at many places in the U.S. and around the world. I was able to track him down via the post office and the telephone company.

Leonard Clarke, Pilot

Often times veterans do not want to be found by military buddies and reminded of the war. Leonard Clarke was such a case. He had given me the address of Eureka, California. All my attempts to reach him over the years had failed. Knowing Leonard, I found it difficult to believe he had moved away from Eureka where all the sizeable Clarke family had lived. Leonard never married but he had seven siblings, all living in Eureka. I obtained an address for a Leonard Clarke who lived in Eureka. I wrote him but received no answer. Several years later, while attending the Dayton, Ohio, Rotary Club's weekly meeting and luncheon, a guest was introduced as being from the Eureka, California, Rotary Club. After the meeting I met with the man from Eureka and explained that I was looking for a POW roommate who lived in Eureka. He told me his brother had just purchased Leonard Clarke's house in Eureka and promised me he would advise him of our meeting and request him to answer my letters. I never heard from Leonard.

Years later, about 1980, I was on an auto trip along the west coast of the country and my route took me close to Eureka, which is on the coast. I arranged my itinerary to go through Eureka. I called Leonard, got him out of the shower, and arranged to meet him at a downtown restaurant for a cup of coffee and some conversation. Much to my surprise, Leonard showed up. I was waiting outside standing along side my rental car when Leonard approached me. He said, "I have been inside the restaurant looking for you. There are a lot of old men who have coffee each morning together. They are all in their eighties and I went around to each one and asked if their name was Lyle Shafer. I thought I had missed you. Then I came outside and here was this kid I recognized as the Lyle Shafer I knew".

Leonard Clarke loved to search for gold. Being a bachelor, he was able to indulge his favorite activity by working at his trade as an electrician until he had enough money to go look for gold. When the money ran out, he returned to his regular income producing job as an electrician. Much of the mining was done in the mountains of Idaho. Leonard pursued numerous lines of work, including being a crop duster, which took him back to his days as an aviation cadet.

Ed Slocum, Pilot

Ed Slocum, a co-pilot, had given me his address as Kansas City MO.

When I arrived at the camp and was ushered into Room 9, there was one bunk left—an upper next to the stove. Seeing I had my arm in a sling and didn't look very frisky, Ed insisted I take the lower bunk and he moved to the upper bunk. A few days later we became the two cooks for the combine. It seems to me we were the cooks for a couple of months, but after reflection, I think it was a much shorter period. It just seemed like two months. I got to know Ed pretty well and after liberation we exchanged Christmas cards. Ed was working in the family's feed and seed business in Kansas City. Later I received a Christmas card from Ed's wife telling me Ed had died. A short time later Ed's wife also died. I later found a son and grandson and met with them. They chose not to correspond with the roommates and there has been no communication with them for years.

Kenneth Frazee, Pilot

Ken's plane was shot down September 5, 1944, but he was not assigned to our room until later when additional men were assigned to the rooms a few months later. I found a family contact listed on the Missing Aircraft Report and consequently was able to communicate with Elaine Frazee, his wife. I was informed that Kenneth had died during June, 1961. He had attended the University of PA and had been engaged in several business enterprises. He had four children and at the time of his death, two grandchildren. Elaine died during September, 1977.

I began communicating with one of Kenneth's sons, Kirk, and the two of us started searching for information about Ken and his crew. We were successful as will be shown later in this book. Kirk and his wife Karen, and on one occasion, accompanied by their two college age daughters, Kristen and Lauren, have attended a number of the reunions held by the POW roommates and are an integral part of the group. It was a rewarding experience for me to find Kirk and his family and help Kirk obtain information about his father for the Frazee family. Kirk has told me on several occasions that inasmuch as he was very young when his father died, he did not know about his war experiences. Kirk believes that through the roommates, he has not only learned to know his father but also he gained a number of surrogate fathers among the roommates.

Harold Speck, Pilot

Harold was a co-pilot on a B-17 flying out of England. He was not one of the original occupants of Room 9 but came in a bit later when the consolidation of prisoners took place. After liberation, Harold and Anita were married July 17, 1945. Anita had just finished college and Harold returned to college. He served as a school principal for a while and in 1952 took a position with Equitable Insurance Company. He died during August, 1987, after a prolonged illness with cancer. Prior to that time, Harold was the victim of a heart attack and had triple by-pass surgery. Unfortunately, I was unable to find Harold until shortly after his death. Anita was a full participant in the POW roommate reunions prior to her death during 2003.

Jack Williams, Pilot

The person I had the most difficulty in locating, was Jack Williams of Chicago IL. I went through the usual steps but could not get a clue. I had remembered that Jack was a member of the 100th Bomb Group which was part of the 13th Group Wing which also contained my Group, the 390th. I obtained the name of the contact man for the 100th Bomb Group Veterans Association and contacted him but they had no such member.

The area where Jack had lived in Chicago had commercialized and no residents were still there. I tried a local High School but was ignored. There are over 5,000 Williams listed in the Chicago telephone book and many of them are named Jack or John. I did not know whether Williams was named Jack or whether that was a nickname. My youngest daughter was working in Chicago at the time and whenever I visited her I would call eight or ten Williams listed in the Chicago telephone listings. I had some interesting conversations but none where of any help.

I became desperate. I had located all my roommates except Jack and the others were itching to have a reunion. I knew Jack very well and the two of us acted as guinea pigs at San Antonio after liberation when the army set up a discharge processing station. I wanted to find him in the worst way. Although Chicago is a huge place, I put an ad in the Chicago Tribune with the pertinent facts and my Dayton, Ohio, telephone number. It just so happened that I was in Chicago at that time visiting my daughter again and dutifully telephoning as many Williams listed in the Chicago directory as I could, when my wife called and stated I had received a response to my ad and a telephone number. The caller stated he knew the Jack Williams I was looking for and asked that I call him. I was really excited and immediately called the number.

It didn't take me long to spot the caller as a con artist trying to make a quick buck. He explained that he could not give me Jack's location because he was running from the law and was in hiding; that the caller was his lawyer; but for $100 he would take me to where Jack was hiding. I told him to give his client my name and telephone number and tell him to call me if he was interested in talking to me.

It has always been my opinion that the key element in searching for people is <u>persistence</u>. A person should keep trying and when all avenues seemed exhausted, start over. I have been told that good detectives go through their evidence again and again if they run into a stone wall. My starting point was to contact the 100th Bomb Group Veterans Association contact man again and ask if they had a member by the name of Jack Williams. He replied "Within the past couple of weeks I received a recommendation from a member to contact a Jack Williams and ask him to become a member of our Veterans Association. I don't know whether he is the man you are looking for but here is his address in Maryland". I contacted Jack and was happy I had found my man. I had found the last of the missing POW roommates.

Jack had remained in the military for several years following the end of the war. A large part of his working career was with Ballistic Research Laboratories at the Aberdeen Proving Grounds. In 1954 he transferred from the Air Force Reserves to the Delaware National Guard.

Don Demmert, Pilot

A few months after we were liberated, Don was living in New Jersey.

On his way to take some music lessons somewhere in the New England states, he stopped to see me for a few moments where I was in college. He was driving a brand new Studebaker car and he was so proud he almost popped a few buttons on his chest. I will have to admit I was envious. The car was the new style with wrap around windows in the front and rear. Singing was Don's avocation and over his working career he honed his skill and used his voice to its fullest. As will be explained in other sections of this book, he also sang for the roommates. During such times you could hear a pin drop—a very unusual condition in a room packed full of prisoners of war.

During Don's working career, Don and I were in contact with one another briefly concerning business. We were both with companies involved with electronics. When I needed to find him I knew I would get a lead from the Chamber of Commerce that included Wayne NJ and I was correct. I later met with Hildegard and Don at their home and they showed me a beautiful 1927 Hispano-suiza automobile they had restored. I was once again envious of their efforts. Don explained to me that the company that manufactured those cars also manufactured airplane engines for WW II.

Jack Murphy, Pilot

The address I had for Jack Murphy failed to give me the connection I needed to contact him and the telephone company was of no help. However, once again, the Chamber of Commerce came through for me. Jack had returned to the Harrisburg PA area and joined his father who was a contractor of road bridges. Jack later was engaged in the building of houses and even later owned and operated the Murphy Building Supply business. Jack and Edythe were married prior to the time Jack was assigned to overseas duties. He spent many months as a test pilot testing airplanes while stationed in North Africa and later requested a transfer to the 15th Air Force in Italy .

Bob Siltamaki, Pilot

Bob often talked of Hanna, Wyoming, his home town. His girl friend Katy also lived in Hanna. Being a small coal mining town, I knew I could get a lead on their address. Bob and Katy were married when the war ended and Bob and a partner established and operated a small manufacturing plant in Burbank, California. I found them through their kinfolk in Hanna, many who still live there. Recently I stopped to visit Hanna and found a small WW II memorial park listing the sons and daughters of Hanna who had been in the war. Bob was prominently mentioned as a P-51 pilot and a true hero to all who knew him.

Glennon Schlueter, Navigator

Glen had given me an address of his parent's home near St. Louis in Illinois. Although Glen and his wife Judy no longer lived there, and in fact had spent a few years working in Germany, there were enough contacts that I could track down Glenn and Judy. Glen was a chemist and the work in Germany was with the U.S. Government, partly dismantling chemical war materials.

Jack Wallace, Pilot

As indicated above, several of the roommates remained in the military until retirement. One of them, and I cannot remember which one, told me Jack Wallace had stayed in the military and was living in Wichita Falls TX.

I met with Doris and Jack Wallace and learned that after his retirement, they purchased a franchise of Snelling and Snelling, a personnel search business. Jack has suffered from a number of health problems and has not been able to attend any of the POW roommate reunions. However, there has been correspondence between Jack and the group.

Carmen "Dusty" Rhoades, Pilot

Dusty had given me a Scottsdale AZ address in 1945. He was married and had lived in Scottsdale for some time prior to entering the military service. My letter to Dusty was returned stating he did not live at that address. I explored the telephone book for Scottsdale and found another address for Dusty. That proved to be the place where he was living. He later moved to Fountain Hills AZ and subsequently back to the Scottsdale address. Dusty engaged in several business ventures including real estate and not long ago he moved back to the address where I found him several years ago. Dusty was a P-47 pilot and had trained at Luke Field near Phoenix.

Coleman Jacobsen, Navigator

Coleman was a resident of Barracks 9 but was not a roommate in room 9. However, he was a friend of Willis T. Jones. Coleman and Willis are both physicians and years later met again at a medical convention. Both live in Texas. Willis practiced in Baytown and Coleman practiced in Dallas. Coleman was interested in the room 9 POW roommate reunions and attended several. Although he is retired from the active practice, Coleman is near the end of serving a five year term as President of the International Dermatology Association which is the umbrella association over the Dermatology Associations around the world. A distinguished dermatologist, Coleman is the recipient of many awards. He travels extensively all over the world to carry out his duties as President of the umbrella association. He is an honorary member of the room 9 POW roommates.

It was amusing to me to hear over and over again the following statement from the men I had just located. "I don't know what the trouble was Lyle, and why it took so long to find me, I have been here all along."

It was only natural that the group started lobbying for a reunion. I agreed to host the reunion, during July 1989, if we could hold it in Dayton, Ohio, where I had spent my working career. Although I had moved after retirement I knew the area and the people who lived there. It was a natural choice. During the time we were there, we attended the National Aviation Hall of Fame Enshrine-ment Ceremonies and was introduced by the Master of Ceremonies John Glenn.

The list of attendees read like the who's who of aviation and was a real treat for the roommates, also aviators. We attended the Dayton International Air Fair and visited the U.S. Air Force Museum. Both were great adventures for the group. The local Public Broadcasting TV station prepared a half hour video of the reunion which has been shown many times over the years. The group was exhausted by all the activity but still had the energy to insist on having a future reunion. Since that time the group has held six reunions hosted in various parts of the country by a roommate and his wife. While the number of roommates still able to travel and attend a reunion has dimished over the years, additional reunions are being planned.

The Experience

Narrated by Elmer T. Lian, B-24 Pilot,
8th Air Force, 34th Bomb Group,

Edited by Erik Dyreborg

Elmer T. Lian, 1943 is pictured above

The Mission Briefing

As a United States First Lieutenant in the Army Air Corps, I was assigned as a pilot on a B-17 bombardment aircraft. In 1944 I was stationed in Mendlesham, England and assigned to the 34th Heavy Bombardment Group. Our mission was to fly strategic bombing missions over Germany and German occupied countries in Europe.

At about ten o'clock in the evening of the 26th of September, 1944 an Army Air Corps soldier entered our Nissen Hut and stated that our crew would fly a mission in the morning. He added that a truck would pick us up outside our barracks at one o'clock.

Our crew was assigned to fly the Boeing made B-17 Flying Fortress. It was assigned to the 34th Heavy Bombardment Group, There were four squadrons assigned to the group; however, our assignments came directly from the Group Operations Office because we were a Lead Crew. The Lead Crews were under continuous combat training in learning new techniques in leading the 36 planes in a combat formation. After flying a typical mission we were immediately sent to a special training base and issued a new plane which incorporated the latest combat equipment. We would train with military and civilian technicians and following a week of training we would return to the 34th Group and lead the next mission.

The day of the next mission, and my last mission, had come. I can recall getting up slowly, because I was tired. I had not slept for many hours and I would get no sleep during the next 20 hours. Having gone through this experience many times, I knew the agony at the end of the mission, of being physically and mentally tired to the point where the muscles, eyes and mind cry out for rest. After dressing, the officers of our crew took turns standing watch outside the door waiting for the truck to pick us up. The base was blacked out so that it was impossible to see any lights or make out any trees or buildings in the cold drizzling rain that was falling. After the truck had picked us up we were taken to the mess hall, where trucks were gradually converging from the remote sections of the base, each carrying a bomber crew. Inside the mess hall we went directly to the long tables and sat down on the hard benches. That particular morning we had pancakes and coffee. A person does not eat very much, "before a mission", he has a funny tight feeling in his stomach and he constantly thinks ahead of what might happen. He also drops back in time in his thinking to what had happened in his past. This could be the day, this could be the last meal, this would be a strange way to end ones life….

Soon it was time to go to the briefing rooms. As a Lead Crew, we went directly to a special operations building and sat down in what looked like a small classroom. The air within the briefing rooms was always tense and smoke filled. At the start of the briefing, the briefing officer would slowly draw open a large curtain displaying a map of Fortress Europe. A fleeting glance at the map registered indelibly on the mind of every man. We had seen these maps many times, we knew all the cities, and we knew where the large concentrations of anti aircraft guns were located. We knew you could not get that red yarn on the map from England to the target without going through hundreds of square miles within the range of enemy gunners. As the curtain is pulled back, your heart stops, your throat is tight, and you grow sticky and clammy. You don't register any emotion, because you're with a team. A number of men depend on you and you depend on them. This is a time in a man's life when he finally realizes that the many months and years of discipline are paying off. Inwardly, he may be a coward, but outwardly he becomes a man of steel and refuses to think of ways of turning back; he thinks of going ahead and doing his job.

On this day our target would be the railroad yards at Ludwigshaven, Germany, a large transportation center about 75 miles southwest of Frankfurt. At this particular hour in history this railway yard was busy sending hundreds of carloads of military supplies into the center of France. This was a big factor in holding up General Patton's (U.S. Army) drive towards the German border. Any detailed explanation of the reasons for the mission, its importance or military value mean little to the average pilot; what is important is his crew, and praying that by luck and faith in 18 hours he will be back in England and in bed.

Leaving the Lead Crew briefing room we walked about half a block, deeply inhaling the cold damp air of the outside, and entered the general briefing room. Here, in a much larger room, about 400 flyers would meet and be told what the secondary targets would be, receive maps of the routes, be shown large pictures of the target, locations of flak (Flieger Abwehr Kanone—enemy ground anti-aircraft artillery) would be pinpointed on maps, enemy fighter strength and locations would be listed, types and number of our own escort fighters would be detailed, escape kits would be issued to all the men. Candy bars would also be given out; two chocolate bars, and one small package of hard candy. There was no lunch on these missions; none was needed or desired. Most of the mission would be at high altitude so one could not eat, and food was the last thing you think of on a bombing mission.

Following the general briefing, it would be about 1:30 in the morning; the crews would head off for specialized briefing. The navigator would get his special maps and time hack (set the time on his wrist watch), the bombardier would get the information on dropping the bombs, the "Mickey" operator would get his radio signal information, and every man would secure his parachute and special gear. On this mission our crew would lead 1500 ships over Europe requiring several special officers and some new combat equipment on our new plane. We had two navigators, one the visual navigator and the other the radio signal navigator. We also had two bombardiers, one would drop bombs under visual conditions and the other was a radar bombardier who would find the target through the clouds. In addition we had the 34th Bomb Group Operations officer flying as a command pilot of the mission in our ship. Finally, we also issued detailed radio code information containing secret words to be used by various lead pilots in passing information up and down the bomber area, sending information back to Bomber Headquarters in London, special words to be used with fighter escort pilots and secret codes to handle emergency situations. These words or statements were in code to confuse or mislead the enemy radio monitoring stations that would be analyzing all the radio information coming from the bomber force. As an example, the words "Red Door" may mean the target area is clear, "High Ball" may mean enemy fighters are concentrating over Belgium, "Apple Pie" may mean to bomb the secondary target rather than the primary. Many times, due to weather, contrails, unknown winds, excessive fighter opposition, the above code scheme would be junked and we would go in the "clear" on all our communications. That is, we would converse in normal language. It should be noted that with 1500 bombers the radio chatter would have to be kept to a minimum and used only by the Group lead ships, and All other ships would merely monitor the radio information.

At the conclusion of all the briefings, you would go to the clothing and dressing room and remove your everyday military clothing and put on your flying clothing. Many thoughts go through your mind as you change your clothes in these crowded and cramped quarters. All of your flying clothing is in a tall upright steel wall locker. As you hang up your shirt and trousers on the hooks and put on the long flying coveralls you take a few meaningful possessions out of your trouser pocket and drop them into your flying coverall. When you finish dressing you usually take a look into some of the other lockers—it's a dramatic experience to open a locker that contained a uniform last week but which is empty this morning. You glance at the names on a couple of other lockers and they are also bare. We all know that as soon as a man is killed or shot down over Europe the Personal Property officer will empty out your wall locker. What they do with your clothes just never comes to your mind. The fact that it is empty blots out your logical train of thought. But you must be getting ready. Someone has called your crew by name and they are waiting to take you to your plane. Just before three o'clock in the morning you arrived at your airplane, after a long drive around the perimeter road on the airbase.

Normally when the crews arrived back from a mission the intelligence officer would debrief certain crewmembers. In a group there would be several hundred men so that it would be impossible to debrief all the men. Consequently, the lead crew of each squadron would undergo most of the debriefing. This activity consists of sitting down and discussing various phases of the mission with the intelligence officer. The navigators and bombardiers would be asked to spell out the exact location of anti-aircraft flak, which was observed. One of the duties of the navigator was to keep a log of the time and place we encountered enemy fire from the ground and fighter aircraft in the air. The bombardier would have information pertaining to the target and how it looked from the air. An hour or two after a raid the U.S. Force Command would send reconnaissance aircraft with photo capability over the target at high speed to photograph or assess the damage.

Preparing the plane

As soon as you arrive at the plane the crew chief meets you and tells you the plane is ready to go. He has run up the engines during the night, had the gas tanks topped off, advise you that the bombs are on board, the oxygen tanks are full, and the flak suits are on board. You will notice the blackout regulations are not as strict here; a few flash light rays will stab the air, the on-board gasoline putt-putt motor is running providing enough electrical current for a few lights inside the plane.

For the next hour there will be much confusion as final checks are made of all the equipment on board. Each man will go to his station and start checking his equipment; the pilots will go through the radio checks, set the altimeter, adjust the seats, check the number of emergency parachutes on board, and perhaps most important, check with the other members of the crew as to their status and problems. The number of flak suits will be carefully divided among the crewmembers because in addition to wearing one each man will want to be sitting on one. These flak suits were made up of pieces of steel disks set in cloth and sewn together to make an apron that would hang over the front and back of your body. These suits weighed about fifteen pounds and provided some protection to small low velocity shrapnel, which would fly out from a flak explosion. Those men who flew or operated in a sitting position usually sat on one suit and draped another over the lap for the ultimate in physical and psychological protection.

Take off and climb

Based on a pre-arranged time schedule, all members of the crew are now in the plane at their stations waiting for the yellow flares, which would be fired in the air indicating it was time to start the engines. In a few minutes all the engines will be warming up and again, in accordance with a schedule and on seeing the green flare, the brakes would be released and our plane would slowly wind its way from its far away parking spot through a number of taxi ways to the end of the take off runway. We would roll onto the main runway and line up facing straight down the runway as the number one lead ship. Then at five o'clock, within a second or two, the double green flares would be fired from the top of the operations building about a mile away. The mission has begun.

Slowly the pilot would start pushing the four black throttle handles forward. The copilot usually had adjusted the tension on the throttle arms to make them hold and feel tight. At about one fourth of the way forward the brakes would be released and the plane would start moving. The copilot would check to see the flaps were down about 30% and that the cowl flaps were in the open position. As the throttles passed the half waypoint the roar from the engine blots out your voice in the ship. As the throttles move to the three-quarter mark the small yellow needles on the instrument panel come to life, and the temperature gauges move to the green, the manifold pressure is moving up, the RPMs (revolutions per minute) are climbing. It flashes through ones mind that it's going to be a long time before these small instrument needles come to rest again.

The throttles are now fully forward to firewall; the halfway point on the runway has been reached; the little lights on the side of the runway are moving by the windows faster. The plane has now reached the point where it no longer is a lumbering object. The controls are starting to stiffen you and the plane are moving together soon to become one and the same. The roar is deafening; you no longer look at the instrument panel to see where the small yellow needles are. Only one instrument counts now and that is the airspeed. You look ahead and can see the end of the runway. There is no turning back; you are committed. You resolve to take the plane off the ground, your prayers are paying off as the wheels and struts are now fully extended. You feel for the light airborne feeling and in that moment you are mentally and physically trying to lift the plane off.

Little did I know when the wheels left the ground that it would be nine years before I would land again in England. Nor did I know that I had begun my last combat mission in World War II. I was totally unaware that I was leaving a way of life and was starting on an adventure that would include some of the saddest as well as the happiest moments of my life.

The sound of the air rushing by the windshield is now continually changing to a higher and higher pitch. The spinning wheels whine as the wheels turn at over a hundred miles an hour. Then the control column is slowly pulled back and the plane leaves the runway. Altitude is just a few feet above the ground and the airspeed indicator slowly moves up. In a second or two the pilot signals "wheels up" and the copilot moves the lever to the "up position". The flaps are adjusted to about 20 degrees and the cowl flaps are closed a little, the throttles are pulled back a little, and the props adjusted in pitch. We are now a couple of miles from the end of the runway and as the wheels hit the up position in the wing you can feel the plane give a little jolt. By now the navigator has begun his work plotting the plane's position on the map by dead reckoning. This elementary navigation system is used to plot ones position or location by using the factors of time, speed, wind and direction.

The next couple of hours are tough. We will have to climb to about 25,000 feet with this full bomb load and the full load of fuel. In addition, one of the most difficult flying maneuvers must now be executed in gathering this giant formation of 1500 planes into a cohesive flying fighting force. The pilot and co-pilot of the lead plane of each unit have it easy compared to the hundreds of planes that must get into formation following the lead planes. This maneuver is basically one of flying a giant circle many miles in diameter, that spiral ever upward to the operational altitude.

The flying of these large circles is also a complex navigational problem because your circle is assigned to a specific air space over England and attempting to keep ones position when flying and navigating while constantly turning may be very hazardous. There would be a number of these large flying circles over England and a most dangerous experience would occur when two of these circles came too close together. The outside ships in both circles would be flying in opposite directions; consequently, head on, mid-air collisions were a part of the game. When you run into another formation it takes 30 seconds before you heart starts pumping blood back into your cold body.

It has now become full daylight. The planes strain to join the flights, squadrons and groups you continually worry about the weather, flak, enemy fighters, and accidents. Last but not least, you worry if this would be your last mission. You think back over other missions and how lucky you were to have made it. You think of the times you have seen bombers break up in the air as a result of enemy artillery hits, and of the dramatic events such as when a B-17 or B-24 has dived straight into the ground from five miles up trailing a long plume of smoke and fire—with no parachutes opening.

The pilots have now been sweating a long time and the arms are sore. The pain is greatest between the shoulder blades from the constant pressure on the control column. In the planes, straining to reach their slot in the formation, the pilot or the person flying is under the influence of vertigo at all times and consequently, can fly for only a few minutes before he must turn the plane over to the other pilot. Vertigo is that state of mind when the visual relationship between your ship and the other plane changes, and you are unable to determine if you are the cause of the change or if it's the other plane. As soon as the pilot releases the controls, takes his feet off the rudder pedals and gets a chance to twist and turn his head so the vertigo will disappear, things will again appear in a true perspective. The relieved pilot will take this opportunity to adjust such controls as the turbo supercharges, cowl flaps, and also take a reading on all the instruments and mentally note those that are off a bit or in the red. The engineer will be standing between the pilot and co-pilot also noting the condition of the ship. The pilot who is taking his rest will carefully watch as the signs of vertigo start creeping over the pilot who is flying. Always the first thing noted is that the pilot will gradually start crossing the controls and the "ball and needle" will slowly move out of synchronization. At a certain point, where the controls become so crossed that the plane no longer has sufficient power to maintain its position, the other pilot will automatically take over and fly for a while. As part of the art of flying one must move the rudder, elevator and aileron controls in a coordinated manner, and if you began moving one control too much you must over compensate with another. This is known as having the "controls crossed".

The crew is now on oxygen with the green soft rubber masks pulled tight around the face, the brown leather helmets are tight, the throat microphone is wrapped around the throat, and the steel helmet is still stowed behind the pilot's seats along with the emergency chutes. The pilots are continually adjusting the throttles to get all four engines synchronized.

At around 8 o'clock the formations have finally formed and now the larger 36 plane groups are starting to merge into a long stream of bombers. The temperature outside the ship is around 30 degrees below zero and the electrical clothing has been plugged in to give additional warmth. The faces are starting to grow tense because in minutes we will start the long turn over the English Channel into Europe. For the next few hours, enemy fighters and flak will soon be a part of our life. You can see the English coast slowly slip away. It looks so peaceful and quiet down there; thoughts come to my mind such as: I wish I were living on one of the farms down there. I would never leave the farm but just sit back and enjoy life by just being alive. You see a little boat on the water and just assume he is fishing. He seems completely oblivious to the many problems and worries we have. No matter what a person thinks about, it seems as if others are in such a much better position than the one in which you find yourself at the present.

To the target

The bombardier, who is watching out the nose of the ship, announces sharply that there is flak at 11 o'clock. The war is on. From now on, luck will be the most important element in the entire world. In front of us will be four or five hours of hell, the enemy will play new tricks, the fighters will be craftier than ever, the flak a little sharper. You pull the steel helmet over your head, and ask the crew to check in on the planes inter-positional telephone system.

Your mind will always be working, thinking, wondering, and fearing the unknown. You think of the mathematical changes, which prove that you don't have an even chance of coming out of this war alive. Your reasoning goes along this line; that 5% of the ships are lost on each mission and you are required to fly

25 missions. This is over 100% loss in the total number of missions. You think to yourself that this is mission number 16—a fairly respectable number and in any group of flyers would stand up well in any conversation. But then again this may be the last one. I wonder what Edwina and my folks would think if they were notified that I was missing in action. They never say you have been killed in this air war. They just send a simple telegram to your wife telling her that her husband is missing in action.

The navigator, Lt. Curtiss Orr from Houston, Texas, was a senior theology student and was about to receive his college degree when he was drafted in the Army Air Corps. He was a man of high morals and one of the most dedicated and highly trained men on the crew. Because of his religious and pastoral training he was always the subject of some good-natured kidding. He took our statements with a "grain of salt" and would modestly call our attention to the great unknown in life. In addition, he was always being challenged to save the soul of some wayward member of the crew when we were on the ground. In the air things took on a different light, the problem of life and death became real rather than academic.

The flak is growing thicker. Some of it is beginning to explode very close. Your eyes are constantly searching the sky for fighters. Someone in the crew will call down to the navigator to pray for us.

For any person who has been in the military service it would be easy to understand the problems that may arise when a crew of 10 or 12 men are welded together in a combat crew. Generally speaking, of course, the officers held positions of greater responsibility and consequently received respect not so much because of who they were but for what they were doing. In my service with aircraft crews, I can never recall an instance where a problem of discipline or disrespect ever arose among any members in a combat crew.

A crew chief, the man that stays on the ground and maintains the plane and prepares it for the next mission, does no fly with the crew. Our crew chief was John Walters from a small town in the coal-mining district of West Virginia. He was much older than the other members of the crew and had a dedication to the plane and crew above and beyond what could be expected from the typical crew chief. He did not live in the Barracks like other men, but slept every night inside the plane and if, for some reason, we did not return to the base he curled up in a sleeping bag on the parking pad. He lived not only in the plane but also with the plane. He washed all his clothes in 100% octane gas, which he drained from the plane. The only time he went to the base was to eat and he would immediately return to his plane on the parking pad. Any man like this is quietly and quickly passed over in the annals of a war, but in many ways it's men like this that mean the difference between a mission that is failed and a mission that is a success. To the men that knew what he was doing he was a hero; to every one else in the military service he was just a crew chief on a B-17.

As we headed into France at our altitude of about 27,500 ft. the contrails were forming behind all the ships. These contrails were a curse. If you could not see the planes from the ground you could see the white contrails. I would think to myself that if I were a gunner on the ground I would just aim and fire at the head of the contrails and, consequently, shoot the plane down. As an added problem we were the first plane in literally an ocean of planes and we were leading 1500 other bombers to a particular target area. If the gunners wanted anyone in particular it would be the lead plane.

Momentarily you think of all the 1500 planes of the 8th Air Force, why should I be flying this lead ship? You are honest with yourself and more than willing to admit there are a hundred other crews that could do just as good a job. A flash of fear goes through your mind. You think to yourself that if you were a German fighter pilot or a German anti-aircraft gunner, who would be your most important target, and the fear persists.

Instantly you are back to your job, checking the cylinder head temperatures. Number two is running in the red and the cowl flaps are opened a little, the air speed is steady at 180 miles per hour, about 220 MPH on the ground. Your eyes quickly read all the gauges and instruments; as long as the needles are in the green it's okay. The navigator calls up and states that the smoke and dust we see at 11 o'clock on the ground is a British artillery barrage by General Montgomery's army who is hammering the German army.

Within a minute or two the navigator announces in his business-like voice that we are over the German front lines troops. The thought crossed my mind that of all the tens of thousands of people on the ground they wished us only one thing and that was—death. Back in the cockpit the navigator was reading off a new compass reading to be made in 90 seconds. It would be 110 degrees. He announced how long we would be flying on this course and what time another directional turn would be made. He would close his announcement by saying that we had 32 minutes to the IP (Initial Point). This occupied an important facet in the terminology of bomber crews; this was the point at which you turn to begin the bombing run over the target.

Flak would be gently puffing the area around you; it don't seem to be coming too close. Just then, to your back, you would see a Flying Fortress turning upside down and go into a steep glide and momentarily you saw the fire and smoke and then a ball of flame and the burning parts slowly drifting towards the ground. We made it a point to note if any parachutes had been seen and if we could determine the plane number or markings. The gunner called out that fighters were forming at 1 o'clock and he could see six of the fighters headed toward the formation. They usually form about 5,000 feet above the formation and then make a head on pass through the formation with all guns blasting. They are coming down, headed straight for the lead group; suddenly they veer off and attack the group to our left, as they pass directly through the group, and in their wake you see three bombers in trouble; one just starts tumbling in the air and disintegrates, another started in a gentle glide down, and the third goes into a flat spin.

On this mission I was obsessed by the fact that I had read in the S-2 confidential file (Air Force Intelligence file) that the German Air Force had built some new planes which did not carry any extra gas or small guns but had mounted a light weight 155 mm cannon in the plane designed to fire a large shell made to explode in a bomber formation and knock down several planes with one shell. In between these thoughts and constantly reading the instruments you prayed strongly that you would survive. Most prayers are thought of as gentle, reserved, quiet, solem and in good taste. The prayers the crew would have were toward a bigger and stronger God than the men on the ground knew. In our prayers we didn't go into details. God himself could see what was going on. I would say that the average prayer, if there is such a thing, would consist of a constant repetition of the words, "Please God, Please God, I don't want to die".

At 9:40 the navigator advised us to turn on a heading of 175 degrees, the IP. We would literally be drilling our way through fighters and flak to the target. The target is that point in space where the bombs are dropped. Within the last 5 minutes we had encountered a thick cloud cover below our plane. No sweat. On this mission we had a graduate student from the Massachusetts Institute of Technology who had brought with him and installed a gadget called a Radar Bombing machine that could bomb through clouds. I believe this was the first operational combat mission to employ the radar bombing technique. Lt. Orr, the Dead Reckoning navigator, and Lt. Donald Pearce turned over the technicalities of the bomb run to Lt. Allen. He advised on the plane intercom that he would drop the bombs on the target.

On the way to the target we were advised by 8th Air Force Headquarters in London as to the wind conditions over Europe and that the cloud cover over the target area was marginal for visual bombing. The target area information had been secured by special reconnaissance planes, usually P-51 or P-38s, which would sweep over a large number of cities and potential target areas gathering weather information and passing this back to Bomber Headquarters. Consequently, target changes could be made at the last minute with reasonably accurate data.

This was Lt. Allen's first mission but he had made hundreds of dry runs on targets and was fully qualified to identify the target on the radar scope and advise the bombardier when to drop the bombs electronically. At 9:42 the tension had reached a high point. The pilot and co-pilot were now flying the ship in direct command of the radar officer who would drop the bombs. Directly ahead of our lead ship I saw four large flak explosions. I knew they were out to get us and I said a quick prayer. Just then I heard a large explosion that sounded like a person had slammed a door in an empty house. I knew they had hit us. I glanced to the right and left and all four engines were turning. Then I noticed number two engine was smoking and in the center of the wing there was a large hole, about a foot across. Then I saw that flames were streaming from the engine and the hole in the wing. This was it. The plane was on fire. In minutes it would explode into a ball of flame. I instinctively reached up and opened the cover on the bright red emergency bell button and pushed it repeatedly, about six times. Everyone knew what the problem was and what to do. It was all over. Now it was every man for himself.

The parachute jump

During my years in the Army Air Corps this was a moment I was not prepared for. No one had told me that a time would come when only one question would be presented to me…live or die. But I had an obsession, and it was to get away from the plane. I had seen so many planes burn, explode, or disintegrate, and in most cases all lives were lost. I wondered what it would be like to die. After the jump bell had rung and as the other crewmen threaded their way towards the exits I felt, for us, "The war was over". I noted on this particular mission I had not been wearing my back pack, so I picked up the emergency parachute behind the pilot's seat, snapped it on, and when all the men had left the plane I sighed a sigh of relief, and pushed my way from the plane.

I immediately found myself in the air with the planes passing over me. It became quiet and still. The change was dramatic.

I could not perceive myself falling through the air. I looked at my parachute and noted a bullet had hit it; the white silk of the parachute was sticking out through the olive drab canvas of the chute cover. I decided I would attempt to open up the chute as soon as possible. If I had any trouble with the chute I could work on it on the way down.

Normally in combat a chute is not opened until you are 2 to 3,000 feet above the ground. But, because of the little trouble that could develop, I opened the chute at about 25,000 ft.

A quick glance up and it looked as if the planes were rapidly going up rather than myself falling. I then pulled the "rip cord"; at once there was a severe jolt, the heavy nylon straps cut into the top part of my legs, the parachute seemed to explode above me. My next words will be etched on my mind forever as I said in a loud clear voice, "Thanks, God". Again I looked up at the waves of planes passing high above me. I saw them waving at me and I waved back in a rather feeble gesture of goodbye. I turned my head and saw the plane I had just left and it was headed down in a steep dive, trailing a long plume of smoke and fire. In the next second it disappeared in the clouds. I glanced in the other direction and I saw three other chutes were open. I wondered why the other chutes did not open or why I couldn't see them. The instinct of the crew stuck in my mind, despite the fact the problem of "life and death" had been received in my favor. In addition to the sights and thoughts described above, the most dramatic change was the utter silence and strange and unreal world that suddenly enveloped me and me alone. I was slowly drifting down through the clouds.

Now I am conscious of the fact that my world had changed in an instant. I must now discount everything I had ever known or experienced. I was going into an unknown world. What would it be like? Where would I go? I was not trained for this; I was not mentally equipped to face this new challenge. It was funny—I couldn't remember what to do? Did they tell me? What had they said? Name, rank, and serial number. This flashed through my mind. I racked my brain and this was all I could remember that they had told me. Name, rank, and serial number. This would not solve the problems ahead of me. When falling through a cloud, the wet mist hits your face, it's funny, and the wind is blowing up. In my recalling I can distinctly hear the Intelligence Officer state at the combat briefing that if you were ever shot down and became a prisoner of war the only thing you had to tell the Germans was your name, rank, and serial number.

I was now falling through clouds. It was misting, wet and cold. I looked at my legs and noted that one of my shoes had come off in the sudden jolt of the parachute opening. My gloves were gone. I had my leather helmet on and my flying clothing. Just then, at about 15,000 feet altitude, after falling for about 5 to 10 minutes, I broke out of the clouds and below me lay my future. I saw a few rivers and streams laying like endless strings of dark blue, I also saw the little roads, houses, fields, and wondered if the people down there could see me. I reached into my pocket and pulled out a Lucky Strike and the old Zippo to light it. The air was cold, damp, and rushing by my face. The ashes and smoke of the cigarette went up rather than down. I looked around and saw almost an endless panorama. It all looked so quiet and peaceful. But I knew better—these people were out to kill me. But putting first things first, I wondered where I would land. Slowly the river and roads seemed to be vectoring in on my fall. That is, the objects such as roads, streams, fields and trees far off seemed to be disappearing, while the roads, fields and so on directly below me seemed to be growing large and I felt like I was in a vortex or eye of a large moving event. I tried to recall what you are supposed to do if you fall in water. I heard a couple of hissing sounds go by and I wondered what they were. Would it be possible that some one was shooting at me? I was already at their mercy, why would they want to shoot me. It was about 15 minutes since I had left the plane, but by now the planes and mission belonged to another world about which I could now care less. I no longer knew that world. My new world was coming up to meet me.

I was drifting down in an agricultural community. I noted several small towns and, to my surprise, I now noted some small cars that seemed to be moving in such a manner that they were boxing me in. I started swaying, but with a little trial and error with the parachute straps I was able to halt the swinging motions. I thought to myself that I had been taught more how to stop the swinging of a parachute than I had on what to do as a prisoner of war. I could see Germans running towards my landing area.

The ground now seemed to be coming up faster, the objects on the far horizon disappearing. Below me a couple of thousand feet, lay a small town and I was drifting towards this village. Now I was soon to hit the ground. I recall the instructions that just before you hit the ground you should flex your legs and relax. I thought I would flex my legs when I was about 50 feet. I glanced to the side and was getting ready for the landing.

My perception was not of falling, but rather the ground was coming up to meet me. Then I hit the ground. "Thank God I am alive and on the ground". My knees had been driven up against my head; my head had been driven down against my knees. Was I in one piece? Had I broken my legs? Could I move? The parachute then, in a rather unceremonious manner, folded over my body. I moved; I seemed all right. I rapidly moved my hands against the pure white silk as I attempted to find an opening. Suddenly I was in the open, the old men with guns, the children with sticks and stones, stood by, posed to pounce on my life. A phase of my life had ended. For a brief moment time stopped; I attempted to smile or indicate, "For me the war is over". My mind just did not register the enemy surrounding me.

Landing in Germany

As I lay crumpled on the ground and after I pulled the chute aside, I saw I was surrounded by a group of perhaps 50 old men, women, and young children. Several of the men had pistols or rifles pointed at me. Some were waving sticks, and some of the men and children had rocks in their hands. I attempted to stand, but my legs gave way because my ankles hurt. For a moment I looked for mercy and understanding, but those days were over, I did not know what they were thinking, but the men waved the rifles menacingly at me, and indicated to me to fold up my chute. I must carry it and get moving. I was again on my feet despite the pain.

By now several of the boys had thrown a few small stones, but the men held them back. I searched in vain for some soldiers, because I felt maybe they would be more considerate. At this time I feared for my life. I didn't know where I would go or what they would do. They had no idea who I was, however, I assumed they knew I was an American flyer. I later learned that had been a false assumption.

The place I landed was a cultivated garden about a block from a small village. There was a freight train standing on the tracks, and they made me walk towards it. When we arrived at the train, they motioned for me to go over the connection between two rail cars, but I was unable to make it because of the pain in my ankles. I crawled under and started limping down a road. When I reached a point about a block down the road, a car approached. I remember it looked like a 1936 Ford. There were three army men in it. They stopped and motioned for me to get into the car. Up to this point I had been followed by this motley group of civilians but I now felt a sense of relief, knowing that I was in the hands of the military.

It has been documented that on at least two occasions men jumped without parachutes and landed safely. One, after falling for nearly two miles through the night to what he imagined was certain death, hit another man whose parachute had just opened and whose body swung out horizontally, clear of the chute. The body must have been at the beginning of its downward swing, or the impact would have severely injured both men. The man who was falling free clung instinctively to the object, which he hit and, finding it to be a pair of legs, held on. His savior turned out to be another member of his own crew. Both came down on the same parachute, receiving only minor injuries.

Another British sergeant fell 18,000 feet with out a parachute and landed on the side of a steep hill in a deep snowdrift. Thereafter his chief difficulty was to convince the Germans, and later his fellow prisoners, that his story was true. To settle the argument, he finally persuaded his captors, the Germans, to take him to the site of the landing and they verified his story by confirming the many details of the event.

Travel to interrogation train

Just before getting into the car, the soldiers searched me and removed all the objects from my pockets and put them into my leather helmet. The objects consisted of two packages of gum, a package of cigarettes, a "Zippo" lighter, and, ironically, my Air Force escape kit. This small escape kit had been zipped up in one of the lower leg pockets of my flying suit. The flyers escape kit was a marvel of ingenuity. It was about the size of two packets of cigarettes laid side by side and contained, among other things, silken maps of Germany, German money, hard candy, fish line and hooks, knife, compass, matches, English-German dictionary, tablets to purify water, first aid supplies, pain killers, pep pills, and aspirin.

After getting into the car we started down the road. During these first few minutes I was concerned about their apprehension. It seemed strange. I noted that I did not seem to be the center of attention, which I sensed to be rather strange. About this time the car suddenly swerved to the side of the road and the three army men jumped out of the car and ran 25 to 50 feet from the car as fast as possible and dropped themselves in the road ditch. It became apparent immediately that this was an air raid and probably fighters (friendly) would fire on the car. The situation then became clear and I fully understood their apprehension and why they were scanning the sky. In about another mile they abruptly stopped again and as they prepared to jump out I indicated that I too wanted the security of the ditch. They motioned OK, so I hobbled out. As I sank into the grass in the ditch next to the car, I felt the strangeness of the situation. All of a sudden I was to attempt to defend myself from the United States Army Air Corps. The world had certainly changed a great deal in the past half hour.

I didn't see any planes nor did I hear any gunfire. I did hear aircraft flying in the area. The soldiers drove about five miles, entered a small town, and stopped in front of a small brick building. As we entered, it appeared to be a town jail with a couple of guards that I assumed to be military police. Immediately I felt that I was the most important character to have entered this jail in a long time. The military police assumed an artificial air of importance and immediately began demonstrating their professional skill to the dozen or so old civilian men who had crowded in the jail to witness the booking of a "killer". The head guard issued orders to his number two man who repeated them to lower ranked guards. They made me stand up and searched all my pockets, which were empty. Then I noted the pseudo professionalism lapse as the guards ran their fingers over my clothing, feeling its quality. The other guards immediately felt my clothing and started talking about its quality. Then the Captain of the guard perceived their amateur behavior and ordered the men away from me. They again assume the air of professional guards. As they sorted out the articles in my helmet they stood in amazement at the strange collection of objects. Picking each one up they felt its weight and smelled the object like children might.

For the first time since I had left the plane I felt some of the intense fear that had built up in me; was not leaving slowly. As they looked and smelled of the F&F (a brand name) cough drops, they concluded that it was medicine and that I had some ailment or that I was sick. After they had placed everything down on the table, I walked up to the table and picked up my package of cigarettes and gave one to each guard and took one myself. I picked up the lighter and lit each one in turn. A mysterious friendly air fell over the room immediately. The sour faces turned to smiles as they savored the rich mild American tobacco as they casually glanced at the unfortunate civilians who were unable to participate in this event.

Following this brief friendship, the Captain of the guard ordered the men back to work. None of them could speak English and I could not speak German but I understood the next order of business. It was to find out who I was. In other words, interrogate me. I repeated my name, rank, and serial number to the guards but they did not understand. After about 10 minutes we all more or less gave up on the interrogation and I sat down. The civilians who had been in the building were now chased out and a new group of men, women and children were allowed to come in and look at the "terror flyer" (Terror Flieger—this was the way the Germans described Allied bomber crew members) that these guards now had in their possession. This was a real live prisoner of war!

I waited about half an hour and then they took me outside to a waiting truck. We all stepped into the back cargo area. It was more or less a freight or express truck. This was a charcoal burning truck with a large tank on the outside converting wood into gas. It had very little power. The only time the driver could get the truck in high gear was going down hill. We went up hills in low or super low. After driving about five miles the truck stopped at a cross road and we all stepped out. The truck left.

Two guards and I started a long march. By now my sprained ankles were really giving me trouble. But I walked slowly and the guards were cooperative in not forcing me to walk faster. They appeared to test me a couple of times to check if I was making up the ankle story, but by rolling up the trouser legs it was obvious I was in pain because the ankles were swollen. Also I had only one shoe but I did have a stocking, which protected the sole of my foot from stones. I saw a town in the distance about five miles ahead, and they indicated it was our destination.

It was now around noon. I had lost track of time. It seemed like days since I had left England and it seemed as if this day would never end. There was a heavy overcast so I had no reference to the sun or to direction. By now I was hungry, but little did I know that the hunger I now felt would be mild compared to the experiences of mind and body that lay ahead.

I was still under the false and unrealistic impression that perhaps I would end up in a prisoner of war camp in the evening and many of my problems would be over. I had never heard my Intelligence Officers talk about what to expect or really what this prisoner business could be all about. I had heard the term Prisoner Of War camp many times, but I realized that what I knew about these camps were nothing more than figments of my own imagination. One fear that started to grow in my mind was that no one in the world knew where I was, no one knew I was a Prisoner Of War (POW), the Germans did not know who I was. Little did I realize that this fact was a well known psychological point used by German Intelligence Officers in their attempts to pry information from us. I rationalized that it really could be no crime for the Germans to kill a nobody. It would be an interesting academic point if I were not involved. I began to think that it was important that the prisoner of war be able to prove who he was. Just giving your name to the enemy seemed so shallow. When I was shot down I had no identification on myself. The German interrogating officers would play up this point to the maximum.

Interrogation train and more travel

As we approached the town, we seemed to angle towards a railroad train made up of passenger coaches. In a pantomime discussion with the guards I understood this would be my destination. I noted a name on the train station but soon forgot it. As we drew near the train, hundreds of townspeople came out to stare and many took pictures with .35mm cameras. From the train several German Air Corps Officers and men appeared and I was turned over to them. I stumbled up into the car and walked through what appeared to be a dining car and was seated in a corner booth.

A German officer approached and after determining that I spoke English, a German corporal stepped forward and asked my name, rank and serial number. He then asked what type of ship I had flown; I told him I was required to give only my name, rank and serial number. I sensed that being given the task of interrogating me was the high point in the corporal's life. The other German soldiers crowded around and he repeated all the questions and answers in German to the men around him. The corporal assumed an air of importance and became very anxious to secure as much information as possible to impress his peers.

At this time I asked the corporal how long he had been in the service and he readily told me. He was a personable guy and appeared willing to talk. Then I asked his rank, how old he was, and again he not only told me but also expanded on his answers. Immediately, I and the other German airmen detected things were not going right. So I asked a couple more questions and he answered. The Germans started smiling and snickering to one another; the officer's face took on a helpless look. Then the officer walked up, abruptly ended the farce, and sent the corporal out. Everyone, including myself, had a good laugh. He was supposed to be interrogating me and I ended up interrogating him. I'm sure he never lived down the incident.

My ankles hurt so I lifted them up on a nearby chair and then I asked for a glass of water, which I received. I waited, and I did not know what I was waiting for. The atmosphere in the coach was relaxed. A German medic came forward, looked at my swollen ankles, and shook his head. The radio in the railway coach was playing the typical heavy beat of German music and I heard the announcer say Stuttgart, indicating the radio station was at Stuttgart.

A few minutes later a very impressive gentleman walked into the railway car. I thought to myself, this is the Gestapo and they have come to pick me up. This is the end of the road for me. No one will ever know what happened to me. This man wore a light green uniform, long black boots, and a particularly dashing German military hat. This so called Hun (the epitome of German self confidence) expressed a nonchalant attitude toward my plight and me. He indicated for me to come with him and we left the train with a couple of military guards and walked up into this small town. I guessed that the Officer was a Colonel by his age and authority; but I was not familiar with German insignia at this time.

They led me to a building about a mile from the railroad car, which appeared to have been a small town schoolhouse. They then led me into a room occupied by a couple of women stenographers and a number of filing cabinets. The guards remained outside. I was seated at a table and the German officer stationed himself behind me. One of the girls pulled all the shades in the room because the townspeople were peering in through the windows. I assumed this was a Gestapo Headquarters or the local police department. The two women were busy typing on some small 3x5 cards and writing letters. While I was in this building, the other employees throughout the building would occasionally come in and view me with about the same expression they would have in viewing a dead body. It gave me a creepy feeling.

During the time I was sitting in this large office, no one spoke to me and it appeared as if I was being held pending the arrival of someone else to take me away. It's at times like these that I kept wondering, where I was going? What was going to happen next? How long would I be here in this building?

While waiting, the two girls in the office opened a small paper bag and ate a lunch consisting of a sandwich. By now food was already starting to play an ever more dominate role in my life. Therefore, my eyes were intrigued by this lunch in an enemy country. The sandwich consisted of coarse dark bread and thick cheese. It didn't look dainty, but it sure looked good and I was in hopes they would give me a little, but no luck. My ankles were throbbing; however, I would not have been in too bad shape if I had not had to do all that walking. In this office, I pulled up a chair and put my legs up on it. This of course helped my physical pain. But I couldn't help wondering what type of punishment they would administer to me.

I thought by now I would have run into some other U.S. Air Corps men, but no luck. I wondered what had happened to the rest of my crew and the other crews that had been shot down. As it grew dusk the apprehension and fear came back because I sensed that I would not be staying in this schoolhouse. Maybe they had decided to take me out at night and shoot me; maybe they would beat me with sticks. I had heard of an incident that ran through my mind often. In England there was a story going around the briefing rooms that one crew which had been shot down over Germany had all been nailed up on the sides of a wooden building in the form of a cross; then the building had been set afire and burned down. My mind also dropped back to my hometown of Fairdale, North Dakota. That was a long, long way from here.

I cursed myself that I had left and I promised myself and my God, that if I should ever be so lucky as to get back there, I would never leave the town limits. What a wonderful little town, with my wife and baby, with so many good friends, and especially, so much good food. I thought they certainly were naïve not to realize how well and pleasant they had it at home. I could see the people, the buildings, the green grass and little gardens, but most of all I could see the table with all the good food my mother would set on the table. I did not realize yet that my mind was slowly changing, and my little dreams would soon become obsessions.

Late in the afternoon, I was taken downtown to the village and brought into a building that looked like a restaurant. We walked up a couple of flights of stairs into the meeting hall. It struck me that it was a meeting room for the Nazi party. The next thing I noticed was that it was dirty, the chairs and tables were broken, and it was obviously not in use. An item that drew my attention was a large picture of Hitler that lay over in one corner, broken and torn. To me, it was an omen of the things to come for the German nation. I wondered if this picture represented the spirit of the nation. Perhaps it was a forerunner of the future.

One of the soldiers brought some food up which consisted of half a loaf of bread and some coffee. This was divided between the soldiers and me. The bread tasted bitter and the coffee rancid, but I was hungry and it was most welcome. I noted that the soldiers ate the food and it appeared that this was the normal fare for them. Therefore, it could be assumed that the food for most people by this time was very poor and meager.

I remained in this room about two hours and it became very dark outside. As I sat there waiting, I was overwhelmed by homesickness, as I had never been before. I did not know if I would live through the night. I became very depressed and everything seemed worthless, useless, senseless, and strange.

Bad Kreuznach Military Police Jail

About eight o'clock in the evening I was taken from the meeting room to the corner of a small street. Here a car was waiting. As we approached, two German officers stepped out and one spoke to me in English. He advised me that, because I was an officer, I would be transported to a Military Guard Unit in the neighboring city, in a government vehicle.

They placed me in the back seat of a car and drove off into the night and into the dark. They had a detached demeanor about me sitting in the back seat. We left the town and I noticed that the paved road became very crooked and started winding over hills and through wooded areas. I could not help but think this was it. They would drive out to a desolate spot and just drop me off and shoot me. No one would ever know what happened to the crew in that B-17 on that fateful day. What a way to end one's life.

Most people can die respectably, and regardless of who they are, at least everyone knows it. But here would perhaps be a case where my wife, child and parents would never know what happened. I guess a guy wants to feel important. After I died it would of course make little difference to me.

As my thoughts ran rampant I did not feel guilty. I thought a man has the right to think anything he wants before he dies. No one would ever know what a coward I was or how afraid I was to die. I recall thinking I should cry, but what a futile thing to do under these circumstances. If I would ever get out of this alive, I was really going to appreciate living. I promised God I would never complain about another thing as long as I lived if I could only be spared losing my life as a result of being shot down. Do you suppose this was punishment for the things I had done in life? But it seemed the punishment was greater than the crime.

During this automobile trip of about 20 miles, my spirits rose a couple of times when I saw a few lights, but when they disappeared my fear rose again. The vehicle was being driven under blackout conditions, which did not add to the mood. Suddenly a group of lights appeared in the distance and it appeared we were headed for a town. Now my depression left me and I felt safe again. To my pleasant surprise the automobile drove up to a large brick building and stopped in front of the door. We all went in and I could see this was a large military police station or police barracks.

A tall, lanky German guard took me upstairs and led me to my room. He could speak a few words of English and said in a laughing way that several of my companions were here in the building. I paid no outward attention because I thought he was attempting to secure some information from me. By now I was very tired and hoped I could lie down and sleep. I also had a sense of safety in the guardhouse.

The room I was taken to was very small and had a high wooden bed that looked like an undertaker's table. On it was a coarse sack or mattress filled with a little straw. I asked the guard if there were any bugs and I recall he said there were all kinds of bugs. In minutes I would have close friends who would stay with me for many months. I was very fortunate in not being allergic to lice, bed bugs, etc. Some of the guys who were allergic would really suffer from the large open festering sores that would break out, particularly around the ankles, wrists, neck, and between the legs.

I asked the guard to go to the bathroom. We walked down a long corridor with cells on each side; to my great surprise several of the crewmembers were there. Immediately I felt less apprehensive. In fact, this was the best I had felt since I arrived in Germany. I asked the guard if I could see all the men in the jail and he obligingly went from door to door and opened it to let me look in the rooms. I counted nine of the crew members in the jail. I was glad to see them and I guess they were glad to see me. We all looked at each other with a cold blank stare, at least pretending we did not know each other.

The guard seemed like a decent fellow and following my return to the cell he brought me a dirty old blanket—it helped because it was cold.

As I lay down I was glad I was no longer a solitary prisoner but at least being with a group of Americans gave me a greater feeling of strength and security. As I glanced around the cell I noticed the door was very thick and the walls were all smooth cement. I always thought jail cells had bars, but I guess that's only in the movies. I wondered what they were doing back in Fairdale, my hometown. I thought of the combat mission fleetingly, and thought, momentarily, of the air base we left in the morning; but these thoughts were now drifting back in my mind. I thought of my family, my hometown, friends, and things that had happened years ago. I just had no idea what my chances were. After lying on this hard, so called bed, for a minute or two I fell asleep. Of course, there was no taking off clothing or other formalities. I just lie down and sleep.

The next thing I remember was the singing and marching of German soldiers outside the building. The soldiers were stamping in union with heavy hob nailed shoes on the pavement. I opened my eyes and it was dark. I thought to myself, poor you, German soldiers and poor me, a German prisoner of war. How strange, how stupid, how meaningless. Life is but a play and I had to go on to the next act as the curtain began to lift slowly.

News report of the raid on which I was shot down

<u>LOSE 49 PLANES IN HEAVY RAIDS</u>

London (AP) in a campaign of aerial destruction rising to its highest pitch in weeks, more than 1,700 allied heavy bombers and an estimated 2,500 fighters assaulted targets in Germany and along the western front Wednesday. Savage sky battles marked the raid and 42 American four-engine bombers and seven fighters were lost. Nearly 1,000 Fortresses and an escort of 700 fighters ripped railway yards and industrial plants at Kassell, Ludwigshaven, Cologne and Mainz with 4,000 tons of bombs. The days heaviest opposition was encountered in this operation by the U.S. Eighth Air Force, whose loss was the largest in weeks, but the Americans accounted for 41 enemy planes, 31 in the air by fighters, five by bombers and five on the ground by strafing.
(Grand Forks Herald—27 September 1944)

From German jail to Interrogation Center

In a few minutes the light came on in the cell and soon the guard opened the door and motioned for me to come. All of us American prisoners left the jail, each guarded by one soldier, and we started walking about 100 feet apart. The name of this city was Bad Kreuznach, population about 10,000 to 15,000. The members of the crew looked fairly good. They were all a little banged up, I noticed some torn clothing, limps, a few scratches, but all in all we had been lucky. Soon we arrived at the railway station and I determined all the crewmembers were present except one officer, but I was not too worried because I knew his chute had opened.

At the railway station I got an uneasy feeling, as there were a number of civilians around and they looked at us rather contemptuously. I knew there would be more stations and more people and perhaps American fighters would subject the train to strafing attacks. As we walked out on the platform the guards became nervous and herded us together. I then sensed the dangerous physical position we were in from the angry, bitter, civilian population. However, the guards, by their action, made it clear they did not want the civilians causing any trouble to these prisoners. As we stood together we continued to act as if we were not members of the same crew.

After waiting about an hour a small train arrived and we were directed into a third class compartment with stiff wooden seats. Opposite from me sat three civilians with lunch buckets and I noted that they all smoked pipes but matches were apparently very scarce. They would all fill their pipes and then use one match to light all three pipes.

That day the sun was shining in contrast to the day before which was heavily overcast. The train moved through an agricultural district. In the fields, I did not see any tractors or horses, only oxen and milk cows pulling clumsy wooden carts and wagons. The work was being done by very old women and men in addition to children from about 6 to 12 years of age. The grain crops had been harvested and now they were in the process of pulling the sugar beets, picking potatoes and garden vegetables. After going about 30 miles, I saw we were approaching a large city. The name on the station was Mainz. I could not recall this name from our missions, but noted it was an industrial city.

As we had approached the city my fear and apprehension mounted because I felt there would be larger crowds, and perhaps this city had been bombed. In a few minutes my worst fears were confirmed when I noticed several large brick buildings burning. The fire was coming out the large upper windows. Along the track I saw the remains of incendiary bombs. Consequently, this city had probably been bombed by the British Air Force during the night. I thought this was certainly a tough spot for prisoners of war to be moving into. The civilians would think we had bombed the city during the night

As the train moved slowly through the switching yards, I began to see the damage and misery caused by the bombers. I saw many railroad cars turned over, engines with blown boilers, tracks that were being repaired, and numerous workmen repairing tracks to keep the trains moving. In the station itself, the windows were all blown out. You could see smoke and fire over the tops of the nearby buildings. Around the depot nurses and doctors were caring for injured and burned persons. The Red Cross had set up a soup wagon and were busy dishing out a light colored watery soup. It looked good but they did not give us any.

We stepped off the train and again were surrounded by our guards who had now put bayonets on the end of the rifles to protect us from the civilians. Things did not look good for us, and I kept wondering if we would make it to our prisoner of war camp. After about an hour we again boarded the train, much to my relief, but it did not dispel my fear, because the train did not move. In about an hour things took a turn for the worse as I heard the air raid sirens start blowing. The only thing I could hope for was that these particular planes would not come to this city. The worst was yet to come. I heard the distant rumble of the American bombers, and when I looked up into the sky I could barely make out the shining specks, which were planes. "My God, My God, why have Thou forsaken me!"

To my relief the bombers left the area and we seemed to have survived another crisis, but not for long. In a few minutes we were herded out of the train and under a passageway that ran under the tracks. We stood in a group against the wall and I knew another air raid was going on. Then, as a climax, the bombs started falling in long rumbling chains of deep throbbing sounds. The tunnel under the tracks was shaking and the bombs were coming closer. After about five minutes of this it occurred to me that the rumbling sound was the passage of trains over the tunnel. I experienced another sense of relief.

We finally left the tunnel and boarded the train and I was happy to be finally getting out of Mainz. The train rolled down the track, into a tunnel, and stopped half way through. Incidentally, it was pitch dark in the train and I assumed something had broken down. The civilians on the train accepted the delay with little concern. After an hour in this tunnel the train backed out and now we understood there had been another air raid. We were taken off the train again at the Mainz railroad platform and herded to the far end of the station platform. We all sat down in a small group and one of the officers who could speak German asked for a drink of water for all the prisoners. A guard walked across the railroad yard and returned with some tea. It was weak, but it was much appreciated. The German-speaking officer determined that we had but a few miles to go to Frankfurt, which would be our camp, and we should arrive there sometime in the evening.

In late afternoon we were finally on the train and on our way. We passed through the long tunnel and then over the Rhine River. As dusk spread I could see we were passing through a beautiful agricultural area. Along the track were several .88mm gun emplacements. It was apparently a gun such as this that had shot down our plane. Along the double track on which our train was moving, I saw boxcars filled with teenage soldiers moving west. Some trains had flat cars loaded with horse drawn army wagons, and long flat cars with mobile emplaced .88 mm guns. These were going into France in an attempt to stop General Patton. I noted with keen interest a large factory built of steel and concrete completely bombed out. I never thought bombing could be this effective. This was just a sample of what I was going to see in Europe. I felt proud, in a strange way that I belonged to such an organization as the United States Army Air Force. They were professionals.

At last, we pulled into a large city, which I assumed to be Frankfurt. I dreaded what might happen in the railway station. As we pulled into this railway station, and again into all the others we had and would be passing through, the first thing I noticed was the hundreds of coaches, box cars, train engines, and other rolling stock burned, wrecked, and full of holes, all compliments of the American Army Air Force flyers. The station itself was a large station, comparable to stations in our larger American cities. It had been heavily damaged. The guards again grew very nervous and put the bayonets back on their rifles. This indicated to me the civilians would be very unfriendly, if not outright rebellious. This assumption was correct.

I later learned that 10 flyers, that is one full B-17 crew, had been hanged at the station by a civilian mob. As we stepped off the train I noticed that every pane of glass in the station had been broken. Glass was piled about 6 inches deep between the rails. The features of the station reminded me of the Union Station in St. Louis.

The guards again moved us quickly from the view of the civilian crowd and placed us at the far end of the loading platform. In half an hour we boarded a local train, which took us to a small suburban station on the north edge of Frankfurt. We were then transferred to a streetcar. After traveling a few miles we stepped off into a cool crisp air of a beautiful fall night.

It was just about midnight and you could make out the outlines of urban houses and small gardens. We could now see our camp about a mile in the distance. I was hoping and praying that they would give us a bowl of vegetable soup. Passing by these small gardens, my mind fancied a large bowl of soup being set before me at the camp.

When we arrived at the camp we were directed into a barbed wire encampment, which contained a number of large army type barracks. Now I was hungry, and I hoped I would get some food. I questioned how long I would be here. I wondered what they would do to me. I was afraid of the coming ordeal.

Interrogation begins

This camp was world renowned for its intelligence activities. Here the Nazi Secret Service had spent millions of dollars and thousands of lives over a period of years in learning all the secrets of securing information from enemy soldiers. Here was the place the intelligence or interrogation officers would use every mental and physical trick to learn secrets of modern warfare from enemy soldiers, which would help the German military cause. The place was Oberusel, (near Frankfurt) Germany, and was known to every Prisoner Of War as a testing area for both the mind and body.

On our arrival we were seated on a bench outside one of the buildings. A German officer stepped out and called out my full name and rank. I was taken into a large office. Another German officer was seated behind the desk. I saluted and he returned the salute. The officer spoke good English and asked me to verify a list of my crewmembers. He told me he was desirous of keeping me with my crew in the Prisoner Of War camp. I said nothing. He then took me into a room with another downed flyer, but this officer was not a member of my crew. This man said he was a pilot and had been shot down the day before. He was very talkative. I said nothing and it became apparent in a few minutes this little trick had failed. He didn't push it very hard and in a few minutes a guard came in the room and called him out.

I had noticed this guy on the streetcar on the way to this camp and wondered how he had all of a sudden joined our crew. On the walk down to the camp he was very friendly and it was apparent to all of us he had been planted by the Germans. I noticed also that this little room was bugged, Microphones had been attached to the under side of the desk.

After the little tinhorn spy had left, one of my crewmembers entered the room. However, we did not say anything to one another. I noted a waste paper basket in a corner. We were alone, and I thought it would be worthwhile looking into it. I pawed through a few papers and much to my delight I found a thick crust of bread someone had discarded. We divided it and it tasted good. I still had hopes we would get something to eat that night, but no luck. Food was most important. Maybe it was becoming my God. My helmet, with a few items, was in the hands of the guards that brought us to the camp.

Again I was called from this room and taken to another office. Here my possessions were laid out on the table in accordance with the Geneva Convention. It was all confiscated with the exception of one stick of Dentyne gum and four F&F cough drops. The guard smelled of the cough drops and determined they were some type of medicine. The gum they kept, but they had me sign a statement to the effect they were holding it and would return the stick to me when I left the camp. Incidentally, they did. The cigarettes were gone, the lighter lost, the escape kit was confiscated by the officer. One of the rules was that any object that had some identification on it which indicated it was U.S. government property was taken away, never to be returned. If it were personal they would return the item.

A guard was soon called and he took us to another building. We walked down a long corridor and stopped at a door, which he opened, and motioned for me to step inside. He then indicated I was to take off my shoe; I only had one. He placed this outside the room. This was a universal policy in all the jails. They never allowed a prisoner to take his shoes in the cell. I suppose the reason was he could use the shoelaces to hang himself.

This was rather absurd in my case because I did not have laces in the shoe and there was no place in the room to tie a lace if one wanted to hang himself.

The little light was on when I walked in, but as the guard closed the door, the little light flicked out. In the brief moment the light was on I noticed a small bed about a foot off the floor. A dirty blanket was lying on the end.

The first thought that hit me was that it did not make much difference if the light was on or off. The only apparent object in the room was a bed built like a shallow coffin with a lumpy straw mattress and a dirty cotton blanket. I just lay down on the bed, dirty, lousy, unshaven, hungry, and homesick. I asked God to please get me out of this. There was not much else to say. To a large extent, my future would depend on my brains and luck.

This was the solitary confinement of the German Intelligence and little did I know how my mind, rather than my body, would now rule my actions. But I had one pleasant thought. I was so darn tired, because for several days I had slept very little. I reasoned I would sleep out my stay in this camp. Little did I know that within an hour psychological forces would begin working on my mind and body.

The first thing was the bed fell down when I attempted to turn on my side. I slowly reconstructed the bed in the dark and lay down again. The first time I moved again the darn bed fell down again. I figured in the morning I would fix it and resigned myself to sleeping on the floor. Quickly I attempted to reconstruct the events of the last couple of days, but in seconds I was sound asleep.

In the morning I was awakened by the slamming of the storm shutters on the windows. It was getting light outside, but I did not know the time. It really made little difference, as the little sophisticated items associated with normal living were things of the past. I lay there, fully clothed, just thinking. Taking off a person's clothes when he went to bed belonged to another world. I had finally become aware I was completely at the mercy of the enemy.

After a few minutes the door was abruptly opened and two small slices of black bread and a cup of German coffee were laid on the floor by the door. As I got up to pick up the bread and coffee, I thought to myself. "This is the first time in my life I have been treated like a dog and can do absolutely nothing about it".

The food intrigued me and I ate the bread slowly. It was black bread, tasty, rich and filling. I wondered why they did not sell this kind of bread in the States. Perhaps when I got back to the States I would start making this type of bread because it was very good. I thought those Germans really know how to make bread. It did occur to me that perhaps because I was hungry, I did not have a good sense of value. What a stupid thought. I had eaten bread all my life and I could certainly determine if bread was good or bad. I was all for the black bread.

I was gradually getting the idea that my values in the world had not been realistic. As I lay on the bed rationalizing my fate and attempting to look ahead, the door again opened and I was called and led down a long corridor into a large office. I noted that I was in a situation reminiscent of an Army Induction Center. Men were lined up at various desks and tables. I was first lined up to have my picture taken by a 35mm camera mounted on a high tripod. The operation reminded me of new recruits being taken into the Air Corps. Then I filled out a card giving my name, rank, and serial number. This temporarily relieved my mind and I thought things were not going too badly. Then I went to a table where a Red Cross worker was seated. She had me fill out a card and advised me that as soon as I was identified this card would be sent to the Geneva Red Cross and my family would be notified that I was a Prisoner Of War.

It should be noted by all readers that at this stage of the game, the prisoner of war is the epitome of ignorance. The enemy, in this case the Germans, was able to casually play on the many facets of a prisoner's emotions that were beyond his comprehension. A thread of thought was now working on me. If the Germans could identify me, perhaps they would release me to a prison camp. But I still had the presence of mind to think that perhaps this was a trick. It could be said at this time that one of the most meaningful items of my prison life was initiated by my writing a little card to my wife, Edwina. The card was simple but I knew there was no one in the world that would write a card like that and that if she should receive it, she would know it was I and I alone.

This little card read:

"Edwina, I'm in good health and feel fine in every way. Don't worry about me. I hope you and Linda are getting along all right. Give my regards to everybody. Love, Elmer."

Little did I realize that this card would be the first and most meaningful message that I ever would convey to Edwina. After writing the card we were ushered into a room with a high-ranking Red Cross official. He handed me a lengthy form and asked me to take the time to fill it out. He added that it was important that I fill it out so he could notify the Red Cross in Geneva and they, in turn, could notify Edwina and my family. At each stage of this indoctrination or reception I had a funny feeling it was a plot to gain information from me. In looking over the Red Cross form I noted they asked a number of military questions such as name, rank, serial number, country, unit, crew number, group number, date of mission, mother's name, father's name, date of birth, wife's name, etc. I turned the form in blank and nothing was said.

Soon I was standing by the door and noted the efficiency of the system. I had figured if a person were shot down he would just be a prisoner of war, but now I saw I was being assigned as a Germany Army Prisoner of War. In a few minutes I was taken back to my cell. I lay down and contemplated the events.

At noon, in the cell, I was given a bowl of soup made of water, cabbage, and alfalfa leaves. I devoured it and said that someday if I got out of this predicament I would make soup just like it. I would make gallons of it and spend the whole day eating this soup. It was rich with a delicious flavor. The taste was perfect. I wished people could realize how wonderful cabbage soup really tastes. But the people back home just didn't know about soup.

In the afternoon, the door opened and the guard indicated for me to follow him. I was led through the building and outside to another building. I entered the large building and was directed to an office. A German intelligence officer, a Major, was seated behind a large desk in this office. The officer, who I shall refer to as an Interrogation Officer or S-2 Officer, invited me to sit down. His tone and demeanor was that of a warm, pleasant, and meaningful man. I saluted him and he returned my salute. The Major asked the guard who had brought me to leave the room. In this relaxed atmosphere he offered me a cigarette, a match, and asked me to sit down. I thought to myself, this is it. I was about to undergo intensive psychological questioning. Now the only thing would be his mind against my mind. I kept repeating to myself; Lt. Lian, you had better watch your step.

The Major, in an offhand manner, asked my name, rank, and serial number, which I gave him. He then asked my duty aboard the plane. I informed him that as a soldier I was under a moral obligation to my country to give only my name, rank, and serial number. He informed me in a pleasant tone that I was correct but that warfare had changed since that clause was written into the prisoner of war rules set forth in the 1929 Geneva Convention. He said it was impossible to establish who I was, just because I was found in a parachute. He said thousands of foreigners were attempting to escape Germany by all known means. He advised me that it was absolutely necessary that I answer the questions he asked, so that he could send me to my permanent Prisoner of War Camp. He also wanted to inform the Red Cross of my welfare. He added that if I did not answer the questions he would turn me over to the German Gestapo, which would not be good.

I was now stumbling mentally and verbally; however my mind was functioning as fast as it could. In a daring request I asked what he had to know. The major said he must know the names of the other crew members, what type of plane we were flying, where we were going, where I was from, my unit number and name, my ship number and markings, and some information about my home base. I again stated that, in accordance with the Geneva Convention, I was obligated to give only my name, rank, and serial number.

His next question was if I had ever studied or read the Geneva Convention rules and regulations covering the conduct and care of Prisoners Of War. I said that the information I had, had been gained from my military training. He said, "Do you know what language the Convention was written in," and I assured him the official language was French. This he agreed to. However, he asked if I had ever read the French version and if I realized that there were many differences in the various languages. Not knowing what to say, I remained silent. At about this point he offered me a cigarette and a match. It was a German cigarette and was what I can best describe as a poor smoke, however, at this time it was most welcome. Incidentally, the package of German cigarettes was laid on my side of the table with the open end toward me, with the implication I could smoke to my heart's content.

Getting back to the rules and regulations governing the Prisoners Of War, the German major advised me the United States translation of the convention differed in various ways from the original. One of the key points was that the original version stated that the prisoner must be identified and that he must give the unit he was from as well as the country. Then he went on to explain that the Rules of Warfare had been written in the time when armies would engage themselves on the ground and at no point did it provide for the identification of airmen who would be found over enemy territory in a parachute.

He went on to reiterate there were thousands of Germans, foreign nationals, slave laborers, and enemies of Germany who did not agree with the German war effort who were attempting to escape by every known means. He knew of several cases where an American had been shot down and a Jew had killed him, taken his uniform, and worked his way into a Prisoner Of War camp. He went on again to explain, that his job was to make a positive identification of me and as soon as that could be established, I would immediately be sent to a permanent camp. He also added that the Red Cross in Geneva would at that time be notified of my status. He mentioned that no Prisoner Of War was reported to the Red Cross until a positive identification had been made.

The major seemed so sincere in his talk and reasoning. He exhibited none of the harshness, brutality, or incompetence one would normally associate with an enemy interrogator. In giving all the matter some serious consideration, I thought of the information they already knew. During the processing routine, I had fairly well determined what they knew about us and me. In one of the pockets of one of the crewmembers they picked up the radio code listings of the groups for the day and it spelled out our home base and type of plane, as well as the radio codes for the day. So if I were forced, I would give him the information he already knew.

At about this point, I thought to myself, I would ask a question. To my surprise the Major seemed anxious to answer and even expounded on the question. I asked when I would leave this camp, and he said just as soon as I was identified. I asked where I would go, and on a large map of Germany he pointed out two possible locations. I then asked how the war was going. He informed me in language that I would describe as marginal in truth, and which, however, I found out later was very close to correct. This was in regard to the northern Rhine River crossing which ended in Allied failure.

The Major asked if any harm had been done to me by any German or if I needed medical care, or if I had any complaints. He now seemed to be trying to build a solid foundation of good will and respect. The Major said that he had lived in San Francisco fourteen years. He had been a manufacturer's representative for a German toy company. During the period when Hitler rose to power he said he felt a patriotic urge to return to the old country and help them in the struggles that lay ahead. He went on to say that following the war he would return to the United States and take up his old job. He said he did not look upon the United States as an enemy, but rather as the innocent victim of a European war.

The interrogation had already taken on the air of something unreal. He was doing most of the talking and explaining. I tried to reason that this was some psychological approach, but it was far too complex and smooth for me to understand. I could only think that I must be wrong in my thinking, but where I could not figure out.

Some of the more subtle reminders of my status were the fact that behind me stood a German guard armed with a rifle. The major sat in an overstuffed chair; I sat on a stiff wooden chair. I was lousy, dirty, unshaven, hungry, afraid, and in total ignorance of what was going to happen next. Although nothing was said, it seemed like such an uneven match of bodies and minds. I was glad to be alive and no one knew this better than the Major, but he would be the last to say it openly.

After about two hours of casual talking, the Major gave me another cigarette and asked the guard to escort me to my room. This room was solitary confinement. It was about 6 feet wide and seven feet long. The walls were smooth gray cement and when the door closed it revealed only a small, pencil thin crack around the doorframe. There was one small window near the top of the room covered by a coarse wire and glass. I now set about to learn to live with myself under the most trying mental and physical conditions. The guy in the next room irritated me a little because he continually sang one song over and over again. He must have sung it 1,000 times—"The Old Rugged Cross". To say he was a singer would be a compliment. Being the walls were thick it was not too loud. I learned to live with it and it became a part of my new life.

There is one fear common to all forms of interrogation and that is the element of uncertainty. Not until a prisoner was questioned did a he realize how completely he was at the mercy of his captors. All the rights a person normally has have suddenly disappeared.

We are so much creatures of our environment that it requires a great effort and will power to retain our personality when the environment is removed. Solitary confinement is like living in a vacuum. When the society of his fellow humans is taken away from a man, when there is no certainty it will be restored, when there is nothing to keep his mind busy, he is left face to face with himself. This fact alone is terrifying when one is confronted with it. Under normal conditions the thoughts of a man move from one reasonable fact to another, but with endless hours ahead and nothing to concentrate on, the mind starts to wander aimlessly to fantastic objects. The same thought begins to repeat itself and seems to come back again like the endless drops of water from a leaky faucet. There is nowhere to turn, either physically or mentally. A man is responsible only to himself and the whole world seems to be against him. Values, which have seemed worth fighting for suddenly, seem doubtful. Truth itself becomes questionable and, in fact, trivial. The prisoners in solitary usually lay half awake, half sleeping, for hours on end. A few had emotional or mental breakdowns in solitary confinement, but the great majority came through the experience with little harm, and just marked it down as part of the game of war and life.

Solitary confinement

One of the first orders of business for the day was to set up the darn bed so it would not fall down. The trouble was that the base of the bed was made of slats and these were too short. There was absolutely no way of making them longer. Under normal conditions a person could have ripped some clothing and stuffed in the end to adjust the slats so they would ride over the sides just a little. I attempted to cross them, turn the bed over and rebuild it, but it was impossible.

At about 5 o'clock in the evening the door opened and two thin slices of black bread plus a cup of warm water were set on the floor by the door. By now food was important. I decided that by eating about one fourth of a slice at a time the enjoyment could last a long time. But once I started eating I couldn't hold back and in a minute it was gone. I had a real good feeling in my stomach and I lay down in an attempt to hold on to the sensation a little longer, but in a few minutes it was gone. I did have one secret weapon in my pocket that would help me more than anything else. I still had the four F&F cough drops. I now had decided that each evening before I lay down for the night I would eat one fourth of the cough drop.

Then in the twilight of the first day, I laid one cough drop on the floor, and with the cup, divided it into four parts. This first day I decided to place the smallest fourth in my mouth. I didn't suck it but just placed it under my tongue where it remained as long as possible. This small cough drop represented a change and a small victory. In a few minutes the storm shutter over the little window was closed and the room was dark.

I lay down in my bed. The old habits of taking one's clothing off before going to bed seemed long ago and forgotten. Nothing was taken off, and as I lay down, I attempted to rationalize the events of the day. The day had been eventful but confusing. I wondered about the other men, what they were saying and doing. But by now I noticed a strange thing; my concern for my crew was weakening. I was becoming more self-centered; it was me against the Germans, against the world. It was me who would have to go through it. No one could help me, not because they didn't care for me, but because they had too many problems of their own. I was beginning to think less and less of the Air Force and I had almost forgotten the event of being shot down. I could care less what was happening back in England. My thoughts were slowly, and more and more drifting towards Edwina, Linda, and my parents. I realized they knew nothing. Some day they would read a cold telegram saying, *"Lt. Lian is missing in action over Europe"*. There was not a thing in the world I could do about it. The events of the future were outside my control.

As my thoughts came back to the cell, I noted it was getting cold and the lice and fleas were beginning to move over my body seeking warmth and food. They started biting. I scratched in the hopes of killing them, but it was a losing battle. I was tired, and in a few minutes I was sound asleep.

Sometime in the morning, the storm shutters were opened and the room became light. During the night the bed had fallen down and I had spent the night on the floor. I had been very tired and hadn't noticed.

I set up my bed again and then I struck upon a good idea. When I was issued the black bread in the morning I would save some and use it to adjust the bed slats so the bed would not fall down.

It was difficult to save part of the bread, but I had to balance this against sleeping on the floor. That bread was really good, and I thought to myself, "If I ever get out of this predicament I will go out and buy or make a lot of black bread and eat it." I realized this was not a culturally middle class food, but people would never find out that I made black bread. Perhaps I could make up some excuse for my wife to leave the house for a day and then I would secretly mix the ingredients and bake the bread myself. After baking the bread I would hide it in an upstairs room. Then I would tell my wife I was tired and I would go upstairs and pretend to go to sleep. I would reach in the closet, take a loaf of the bread and eat it.

It seemed funny, but Edwina would just not understand. She did not live in a real world. Only I knew what was good and I could not deny myself the treasure and pleasure of the wonderful black bread.

As the day wore on, I heard a bell pealing approximately every 15 minutes. I could not figure out the time exactly. As this bell rang at first it seemed some type of a psychological trick to lengthen the time and to drive a person nuts. I walked a little in the room to get some exercise, but those ankles still hurt. They were swollen. Little did I realize that many problems lay ahead with the legs. In solitary confinement, I lay most of the time so the swelling would go down, and I did not have too much trouble or pain.

During the afternoon, I recalled the Major said he would talk to me the next day. The afternoon had begun and I started waiting and waiting; supposing something had gone wrong. Maybe I had been scratched off the list. Maybe something had happened in the war that had changed all. By now I was anxious to talk to someone. A certain nervous tension was building up in me. I could not explain it but I wanted somehow to express my emotions to somebody, somewhere, somehow. You don't suppose this is all a part of some big scheme?

Soon I was given my supper and the shutters were closed. I felt fairly confident of the evening and night. I had made my bed more secure, and I did have the thought that being I had dozed on and off during the day, perhaps I would not sleep well. A day earlier I never thought I would get caught up on my sleep, but now I was wide-awake and thinking. In my position, it seemed self evident that God had forgotten me. There were so many people in the world for God to think about and I was so unimportant.

I slept a little during the night and towards morning.

When the shutters were opened the next morning I thought today I would be interrogated again and, perhaps by nightfall, I would be on my way to a prisoner of war camp. The Major had made it very clear to me that until I was identified; I was not yet considered a Prisoner Of War. I was just an unknown individual. This bothered me a little.

During the day I hoped I would be called by the Major for further interrogation. I began to think I knew much less than he did and even if I told everything I knew, he would learn nothing new. For some unknown reason I had a strong desire to express myself verbally and emotionally. I lay back on the bed. The bed consisted of a thin mattress filled with a little straw and a dirty light blue cotton blanket. It was not a cotton blanket in the common sense but very coarse material. I was thankful for anything.

The nights were cold and I was cold and hungry. On the wall was a small handle. When it was turned a small flag fell down outside the cell and the guard would come to the cell. The only time you turned the handle was when you wanted to go to the washroom. In the late afternoon, I turned it and a guard took me to the washroom. The wash room consisted only of a pail in the corner, no water, no paper, no mirror, no nothing. These little items have a tendency to degrade a normal person, but living had now become a question of fate and chance. The niceties of life were a long way in the past.

As night fell, the cold, the hunger, and the lice—all were now working. The storm shutters were closed.

As I lay on my bed my thoughts, of course, would roam far and wide. What would Edwina think when she found out I was missing in action? Linda, the baby, only three months, would not understand. I knew it would be mentally hard on my father and mother. These thoughts kept coming back to me and would interrupt any other thoughts I would have. I could take care of myself but some people were depending on me. My daughter, Linda, was my responsibility and here I was, unable to give her even a smile.

At this time in the evening, my morale would be at a low ebb; the unknown prisoner in the next cell singing The Old Rugged Cross, the lice biting. I made a dramatic move to aid myself. I reached into my shirt pocket and pulled out the one fourth of an F&F cough drop and ceremoniously placed it under my tongue, realizing full well that this would be the most pleasant thing to happen to me today. The sweetness, the aroma, the taste, the only joy I would know was now at hand. As it rested under the tongue I savored the beautiful taste. How lucky I was to have been able to save the F&F cough drops. Some day I would buy a barrel of F&F cough drops and I would put 5 or maybe 10 or 20 in my mouth at once. I couldn't do this around my friends, but I would do it when I was alone. My friends would not know how wonderful F&F cough drops tasted.

I had decided I would treat myself to one fourth of an F&F cough drop each day. This would be the last thing in the evening. It was in the evening that I became depressed. I felt useless. I felt like I was a failure to somebody, in particular to my wife, Edwina, Linda, and my folks.

I couldn't help thinking back to Seymour, Indiana. This was the base at which I had received my Silver Wings at the completion of the pilot training program. We received our wings in the morning and in the afternoon we received our orders. My orders read that I was being assigned as an instructor in B-17s in Boca Raton, Florida. I was extremely disappointed. I immediately went to headquarters and vigorously protested my being assigned as an instructor. I wanted to go to combat. This was where the men went; the boys stayed in the States. After much persuasion they changed my orders to a combat group in Salt Lake City

At this time, I regretted my decision, but I did not look back at myself as being foolhardy. I wanted action and I received action. It was my own choice. Fate perhaps had more to do with the whole set of circumstances than a wrong decision. Here I was and there was no turning the clock back. I would have to go ahead.

As time passed, I would occasionally take a survey of myself. I was dirty, I had not had my clothes off for days, the number and day of the week were no longer important, I was cold, the lice liked me and I could feel them nibbling on my wrists, neck, hair, and waist. My unshaven face felt itchy, my ankles were now in fairly good shape, and lying in bed, they did not hurt. I was continually obsessed by the idea that no one in the world knew of my situation. Back in Fairdale, my family assumed I was busy flying over Europe.

Fitfully I slept the night out. When I first had entered the room I had felt confident that I would sleep out the war. Now my days and nights were mixed up, and I couldn't tell if I was daydreaming or sleeping. I was always half awake, but soon morning would come and one of the emotional high lights was the moment that the shutter was opened on my window and the light of day would replace the dark of night. Soon there would be breakfast. I longed for the black bread and the warm so-called German coffee. In my simple taste test analysis, it was my opinion that the coffee was made from roasted barley. It tasted good. To this day I am sure I was right.

There was a small sign in the room, nailed on a wall near a door. It was about one inch by two inches and it read, in English, "Any prisoner found guilty of writing on wall or damaging property will be severely punished". I did note, however, that a few things were written on the wall, for example: "…V", "Victory", "Give only your name, rank, and serial number", "This cell wired, keep quiet", "Don't open your mouth", "Watch your step", "Home by Christmas", "Two more months", etc. Outside, the stupid bell kept ringing every fifteen minutes and I could not figure it out. It just seemed to make the time go slower, but then, so what. I really did not care what time it was.

As the days passed I noticed my mind was growing a little "fuzzy". My perspective of events and objects was slowly changing, and I thought how little people understood or appreciated. I became obsessed with the desire to talk to someone, or just to see someone; I had a strong urge to find out what was happening in the world. Food had now, in a sense, become a God. Little objects like a bar of candy assumed giant proportions in my mind.

I was aware of what was happening, but I kept repeating to myself how stupid I was never to have realized these things before. I was not crazy, but I thought how the men back in the States or at the base were wallowing in food, drink, and warm clothing. They just did not realize how good they had it. I also thought how little they knew about what was happening in the small cell somewhere in Germany, and how lucky they were.

The German Major questions me again

While in the camp, I had not seen any other prisoners; I was in a world alone. The guard that took me to the toilet or wash room was just a worker and I immediately sensed he felt sorry for me and I felt sorry for him but I could do nothing about it. As an example of the rapport I had with my guard, when I was interrogated the first time, I had stolen (God forgive me) a couple of cigarettes, but with no matches, the only way I could get them lit was to ask the guard for a match when I went to the wash room. In every case the guard would produce a match. There was a deep understanding that if he cooperated with me and gave me a match, I would cooperate with him. By the way, the guard was old; perhaps 70, and he had a pathetic look on his face. The Germany he knew with beer, song, God, love, and savory food had long gone because of the war.

In the afternoon of this 3rd or 4th day in solitary, I started having the feeling that they may have forgotten about me. But, late in the afternoon, the door opened and I was called by name and rank—the Germans were religious about rank—and the guard indicated for me to come. I was brought back to the same German Major. Our greeting was friendly and proper. I felt I had survived the first interrogation and this would be number two. Perhaps, if all the points could be cleared, I would be on my way to my permanent camp this evening.

The Major pulled my file from the desk and unfolded the manila folder. He offered me a cigarette and a match. I could not think of a better way to start an interrogation. In this session, rather than starting off with questions, he first stated that Germany was not angry at the United States. He said the Jews and Russians were trying to gain control of the world. When speaking of the United States in particular, he stated that Churchill and the Jews had talked the United States into going into war.

I asked where he stood on the question of the Italians, who were then a war ally of Germany. He said the Italians were no good and the only reason Germany had Italy on her side was to help the German war effort. I then asked him about the

Japanese. He said the Germans hated them almost as much as the United States did. The only reason Germany had talked the Japanese into the war was to help the German war effort. Another question I asked him was when the war would end. He said it would end some time during a period from May to July of 1945. He said he did have some faith in Hitler's secret weapons or perhaps there would be a break between the Allies which would turn the tide. When we were speaking of the war ending, we both assumed it would end in the favor of the allies. This was strictly an assumption on my part.

I asked how much longer I would be in this camp, and he said, just a couple more days. He wanted to clear up who I was, and explained to me that I would not be released until I had been fully identified. He went back over the same questions we had discussed before. At this time he also explained that it was his duty to fill out a form on each prisoner and he was under instructions not to have the prisoner released until the form was filled out. So, as far as he was concerned, the matter was cut and dried. He had a job to do, and, of course, as a military man, would do it. In other words, if I failed to live up to my military code I would be released. If he failed to do his duty he would face a military court martial. It was a question of one man against another. He implied to me that so far he had never failed and he had no intention of letting me become the first exception. The session, at this point, ended abruptly and I was sent back to my cell.

Back in my solitary cell, I was able to contemplate in detail all the questions and answers in the discussion that had taken place during the two-hour interrogation. I was really unable to plan ahead or scheme any sort of strategy. I would just have to play it by ear when I was called again. I still had not seen any other prisoners, and the only person I was aware of was the guy in the next cell, who never, for a moment, stopped his monotonous singing of "The Old Rugged Cross". The fleas were biting a little harder as I lay on the hard mattress in the afternoon thinking. My face was sore, the ankles ached slightly, my body was growing stiff from lack of exercise, and the little black bread I had, I was now rationing to myself on an hourly basis during the day. My mind was slowing down and one thought kept coming back to me over and over. "I have got to get out of here." I realized that this was just what the Germans wanted and they had me just where they wanted me.

Up until this time it had never occurred to me that they were leery of all my actions and behavior in camp. I had just assumed that I was an ordinary, average Air Force pilot shot down in Germany, and, to be realistic, the German Major knew a lot more about our military operations than I did. The major had, to date, never let on to me that I seemed to be a key. They were very much concerned about who I was and just what I was doing.

The crew composition was very odd. From a casual interrogation of the balance of the crew, they had determined there were three pilots on board, three navigators, and two bombardiers. These figures were far in excess of a normal lead crew and the crew composition was the most unusual they had ever run into, so here was something, but what they did not know.

The plane had been completely demolished in the dive straight into the ground at 800 miles per hour. This fact was verified by a gunner who had landed near the plane. I had never stopped to consider these facts. Of the 1500 planes flying on the raid, we were the number one crew and it could be reasonably expected that we had things on board unknown to the German Air Force. These facts had slipped from my mind. To me, I was just one of the 400 men shot down that day. The Major, of course, implied to me that I also was just an average pilot and that his questioning was routine.

Every night before I thought I would go to sleep, I prayed as best I could. If sincerity is an element of prayer, I should certainly receive an A for every night. Sometimes, in the daytime, I prayed, but I had been used to praying at night, and it seemed rather sacrilegious to pray in the daylight. Also, in this position, your prayers seem rather weak because you have nothing to offer in return. You are helpless. I was but a grain of sand on the beach of life.

The next day the routine was now becoming familiar. The two thin slices (and I repeat, thin slices) of black bread and a cup of barley coffee were set on the floor just inside the door. Obviously I was hungry, but my basic instinct held sway. It was still a matter of life and death to me. I was still a nobody.

This was about the fifth day and I thought to myself, the United States government perhaps has now notified Edwina. A fear flashed through my mind.

Food, home and doubt

I was aware that, to date, my family at Fairdale had been living in relative bliss and knew nothing of what had happened. Any day now the burden of tears, love, concern, and anguish would shift from this little cell in Germany to the little town of Fairdale. This I feared. How would Edwina react when she received the telegram delivered to her large brown house? The depot agent, after receiving the telegram, would perhaps go uptown to seek out her father and mother and advise them first. Then, in minutes, they would carry the little yellow telegram down to Edwina. What would they say? Would they let her read it and then put their arms around her? What would her reaction be? What about Linda? Would Edwina run and grab Linda and hold her to her breast while she sobbed? Life and death are realistic and dramatic.

During the day, in the cell, I had taken off my clothing and searched very closely for lice. I found about three dozen and I killed them. The lice in my hair I could not find. I had gone without a comb for about a week and my beard was long and itchy. I must have looked horrible. I had not brushed my teeth; my bathroom habits had left a lot to be desired. It was no longer a question of niceties; it was a question of life or death.

The bed was causing me problems but I had, by now, learned not to move at night. In six days my clothes had become part of my body because I had not taken them off. My values were changing.

After a couple of days of wondering and waiting, I was finally called, about the seventh day, to be interrogated again. The Major was again always proper—and the package of German cigarettes was again lying on the desk near me. He would pull out the folder with my name on it and quickly check the items he was looking for. He reiterated that he was extremely anxious to have me identified and to have me released from the camp because other prisoners were coming in and the camp was filling to capacity.

Somehow the question came up as to what happened when the camp filled to capacity. He emphatically stated that the overflow of unidentified prisoners would be turned over to the Gestapo. In talking about the Gestapo, he only said he did not know what they did with the men turned over to them, and he never heard any information as to what happened. He led me to believe they were killed. This was not an unreasonable deduction. He asked me to carefully and prayerfully consider all the alternatives and what the consequences would be. Again he went over his job, his duties, and his mission. He advised me that each day a briefing was held to assess the information gained during the day to determine if the prisoner had been identified and if he should be released. He spoke of our mutual problems and asked me to be reasonable and judge my life against the little information I could give.

I was taken back to my cell, which by now had become home. I was, by now, constantly hungry. I was beginning to have lurid daydreams of food. If I ever got out of here I would eat and eat and eat.

The last couple of days, by an ingenious scheme of climbing up on the bedstead and the wall, I had been able to look out the little window in the top of the cell wall. To my surprise the window looked out over a small courtyard. In this yard the Germans were busy digging holes about four feet deep and filling them with potatoes, turnips, cabbage, carrots, and other garden vegetables. After the hole was filled they put straw over it and put about six inches of dirt over the straw. I recognized this as an excellent manner for storing garden vegetables for the winter. I saw the small carts being pulled into the court by a cow or ox and then unloaded. It was an indication of the poverty and desperation of the country. What went into these holes would be the soup for the Prisoner Of War during the winter and spring.

Life in the cell was wearing me down continually. When will I get out? Where will I go? What will they do to me when I do get out? How will I go to that "somewhere"? There were a thousand questions and not one answer. I still had not seen another prisoner. I felt very much alone.

I no longer thought of my crew, my unit back in England, my Army Air Force, my training, and associated things. My thoughts were gradually being concentrated on my wife and baby and my folks. I was taking care of myself, but I felt they could not take care of themselves until I arrived in Fairdale. The trouble was they would not know what was going on and, consequently, their imagination would run rampant with horrible thoughts of beating, torture, and suffering. Here I was and could do nothing about it.

God, if I could only get out of here, I would reorient my life totally in other directions. First of all I would never leave home. I'd live on a little farm with a garden and I would raise acres of vegetables. Vegetable soup would be wonderful.

I tried to walk a little in the cell to get some exercise but my body was getting stiff, and what was the use of walking. My principal activity was thinking. I was attempting to think through my problems. I never dreamed I would get into this kind of a predicament. I had to sort out my thoughts so I could make it. Sometimes I felt like crying but I never did—it would have been useless. I thought to myself, perhaps the only time a person would cry was when there was someone to listen to him. To express one's inner emotions to oneself seemed so empty. Life went on in the cell. I still had a couple of the little F&F cough drop parts left and this would be my strength when night fell. It was when it got dark that my emotions fell to the lowest ebb. Boy, did I ever get homesick. I literally ached all over my body when my dreams took me home to my family.

It was now the tenth day and my doubts about almost everything were beginning to waver. Perhaps there was a lot more going on that I knew nothing about, perhaps. But I had no idea what it would be. During the last interview the interrogator had made it a little clear that I appeared to be a big question mark in his mind. He said that from the German intelligence files, it appeared I had not been promoted as fast as the other men. Consequently, I may be a little dissatisfied with the Army Air Force. He said it a little more subtly, but it appeared I had not had as many opportunities as the other men on the crew. The implication being that maybe I had been cheated by the United States government. He was trying to see if I had any complaints against the service. I made it very clear that I was well satisfied with my Air Force career and the way people had treated me. I did not know it, but they still were trying to determine what I was doing on the crew.

A rather strange experience took place near the very end of my interrogation at Dulag Luft, when the intelligence officer pulled out a new Army Air Force identification card with my picture on it. What made it so strange was I had taken the picture about a week before I was shot down and, as yet, had not been issued this new I.D. card which, was already in his possession. How he had come into possession of the card is beyond me. One of the ideas I had was that all the pictures in the Group had been reproduced and some traitor had thrown the package with all the new cards from a plane flying over Germany. Apparently they had sources of information that had never been explained to me by my intelligence officer. If he could get my picture out of the intelligence officer before I could get it, there apparently were forces at work beyond my comprehension. This fact was discussed and debated among various members of our crew and we could never arrive at a logical conclusion.

Final interrogation

Little did I know that on the afternoon of the tenth day I would have my final interrogation. The guard came and called me. By now my hair was just a mat of lice and bugs, my beard was long and itchy, my hands had turned kind of shiny from never being washed, my clothes had become part of me. I smelled bad but I could not detect it, and if I did, so what. My thoughts were I wanted to get out of this place. My emotions had now been turned down low and I was depressed. I was getting used to being fed and treated like a dog. The washroom facilities were particularly degrading, but it was becoming part of my life. I must say my guard, who constantly marched the long corridors, was considerate and very human. I had built up a sort of rapport that worked well with all the guards. They changed often so I would not see the same guard but perhaps once every two days. Language was not a barrier for the looks in our eyes spoke of all the trouble we both had. I felt sorry for him and he felt sorry for me. Neither of us could do anything about it. One of my overpowering emotions was that of loneliness. I wanted desperately to express myself to anyone who would listen. I just could not see this as a scheme by the German intelligence people. How in the world could they ever understand what I was going through because they had never gone through this solitary confinement.

As I entered his office, the Major offered me the customary German cigarette, which I most appreciated. However, I attempted to smoke it with a detached look and outward feeling as if to say it made little difference to me. His first statement was that I would be leaving camp tomorrow. I had no reason to doubt him and I felt a surge of excitement and relief. He added that, in my case, always addressing me as Lt. Lian, everything from now on would be all right. These were beautiful words and it warmed my heart as nothing in my life had. To add to my good feeling, he said when I got to my permanent camp I should read as much as I could about the German culture and he begged me to understand the German people, adding they were not as bad as I had been led to believe.

As I snuffed out the cigarette and surreptitiously placed another cigarette in my pocket, the Major reached for a large drawer. From this drawer he pulled a large loose-leaf book. It was about 12 by 18 inches and contained about a hundred pages. On the front was the familiar 34 Bomb Group insignia. This book held the secrets of the German Intelligence concerning the Group. The major said that they had been able to gain a great deal of information concerning our Group in the past.

He said one quick method of identification he would ask me was to name some of the crews that had been shot down during the past months. How reasonable he was, how stubborn I had been. I could not see anything wrong with this so I named three or four crews. He said yes, he had them in his book. He looked up one of the crews and then turned the book over to me and asked me to look through the book. As I turned from page to page I noted that he had a complete tabulation of every crew that had been shot down; the mission, the crewmembers, their position in the ship, type of aircraft, special equipment. I noted he did not have the correct identification symbols on the airplane tail. He also knew this was wrong and asked me to correct it on the form. I corrected what he had but I made it wrong; I noted the other persons had also corrected it in error. He didn't know.

When he was asking me, he was thinking of his German commanding officer. I could sense he wanted to go to his commander and state that he had an officer who had corrected the tail markings. To the best of his knowledge, it was correct. He did question me closely as to who my Air Force commanding officer was. I told him I did not know. He felt I was lying, but pursuing the matter further, I advised him I was away from the group almost all the time and I could care less who the commander was. I told him who had been and he verified this in his book. Then he told me who the current Group Commander was and I could only say that he was probably correct. My status on the crew was still in question but he had to give up on that matter. He knew I was a pilot but just how I fit in was the question: was I the pilot, command pilot, co-pilot, or what? On this mission I had been the pilot, but he still had dubious thoughts for he could not unravel the crew positions.

I also detected he had another pilot to interrogate and I would be leaving, so he had to complete his job as rapidly as possible. I recall as the Major and I separated, he asked me if I had read many books while in camp. I said I had no books. He said, "If you had just asked me I would have provided all the books you would have wanted". He added, "Have you been mistreated or harmed in the interrogation?" I said, "No." (Please let me get out of this place.) The guard came to attention when he called and I was led back to my cell. Was this the end? I thought so. I hoped so. I prayed so.

The guard brought me back to my cell and I assumed I would be leaving the next day to my permanent camp somewhere in Germany. I could not be certain. To my great relief, the next morning I was called from my cell and noted several other prisoners gathering at the end of the corridor. In minutes we were taken outside-a group of about 50 prisoners. There were four or five British officers in the group. Standing outside that cool morning, the German officer read off the roster of officers and returned certain items of personal effects that had not been confiscated. When he came to my name, I stepped forward and he gave me back my stick of Dentyne gum. The Germans were very proper and orderly on many things. I had noted by now that they had a great deal more paper work than in the U.S. Army Air Force.

As a closing thought concerning the interrogation process, it should be noted that I, as a prisoner, would be in a poor position to make an overall evaluation. The enemy had all the cards, all the skill, and knew all the rules of the game. The prisoner is at a distinct disadvantage and has very little to fight back with or to compensate for his inadequacy. Looking back, I think that lying, coupled with the prisoner's inherent ignorance, would present the most trying obstacle in the path of an enemy interrogator. Misleading information is difficult to deal with because it will cause more confusion than would mere silence. It must be remembered the enemy already had a great deal of information and the interrogator sooner or later would let you know indirectly just what information he is looking for, and if the prisoner is smart enough, he might be able to play this fact to his own advantage.

The above thoughts are obviously very personal and would be contrary to the old name, serial number, and rank game. The old rules give the interrogator too much leverage and he can apply too much pressure on the lowly prisoner.

From Interrogation Camp to Wetzlar, Germany

After leaving the Interrogation Camp we marched, or I should say hobbled, about three miles, to a small town railway station. One of the prisoners had determined from the guard that we would be going about 50 miles to the town of Wetzlar, Germany. This place was referred to as a DULAG, meaning transient prison camp. I really did not understand what I would be doing in this camp. We boarded a local train and moved, with a number of starts and stops, the 50 miles through the beautiful countryside. As we passed over two bridges, which had just been bombed, I saw my first Russian prisoners of war. They were being used as laborers in repairing the tracks. The tracks had been damaged in several places, and also many old civilians were busy restoring the railroad bed and track.

The group of prisoners that rode the train that day was a strange, motley group of men. Some limped, some had bandages; some were missing items of clothing. For example, I still had only one shoe and my ankles still bothered me so I limped. None of us had shaved, none had hats or caps. Our hair stuck up in unruly mats of disarray. It was noted that the men were all relieved to leave camp and felt a sense of safety in being together with other Americans.

Arriving in Wetzlar, I noted a large factory across the street as the manufacturing plant of the Leica Camera. The camp was on a hill about a mile away. We moved up the hill, and again went through some sort of processing. This was heaven. We were each issued a small Red Cross parcel. In this paper box was a razor, soap, towel, underwear, socks, a toothbrush, and two candy bars. We were assigned a barracks. We took our first shower and shave in a couple of weeks. In the evening we were called to a large dining room where we were given some food. When we had been seated in the hall the German officer advised us that we would be here a day and would depart for our permanent camp tomorrow. He insisted on correct behavior and discipline from all the prisoners.

Our meal consisted of a small can of tomato puree. It was really wonderful food. Following this meal, an English Chaplain stood up before the group and spoke a few words concerning our behavior and conduct in Germany. I guess he was a permanent prisoner of war the Germans kept in this camp to help the Allied prisoners get off on the right foot.

German guard speech

The next afternoon a group of about 100 Prisoners Of War was assembled in the compound. We were advised that we would leave that afternoon for our permanent camp. It was at this time that the senior German officer would make a speech to the prisoners. I should say, the senior German officer who could speak English. By now I had heard the speech several times and I would hear it again. In many ways it was a memorable speech in that it summed up the relationship between the German people and the prisoners. The speech is quoted below, to the best of my memory:

> "Gentlemen, you are prisoners of war, and will be treated in accordance with the Geneva Convention. You are to depart Wetzlar and go to Barth. The senior German officer is your commander, and he has orders to deliver you dead or alive. He will fulfill his orders to the utmost.
>
> You must remember you will be walking through the streets of towns and cities in which the majority of the people have lost most of their earthly possessions, lost most of their future, lost friends and loved ones. These people are very bitter against you men of the Air Force, more so than anyone else in the world. They are easily aroused; therefore, do nothing to incite them. The guards have orders to protect you. Do not sing, laugh, talk loud, or do anything that may arouse the civilian population.

According to the Geneva Convention you must be warned before you can be shot in your attempt to escape. You are hereby warned and therefore, no further warning need be given as long as you are Prisoners Of War.

You are soldiers and Prisoners Of War; you will salute all German officers senior to yourself. You will obey the orders of all guards regardless of rank. The interpreter and medical first aid man on the trip will be............, the senior Allied officer will be Captain.............That is all."

Train ride to Barth, Germany

Just prior to leaving, each prisoner was issued a Red Cross package of food. This would be our food for the journey. In the late afternoon we walked down to the railway station and boarded our special railway car. I believe the car, or coach, was made to hold about 40 men but we had over 100 men in it. On the top, in large white letters, were the initials P O W.

This would be a long, difficult ride. We were very crowded and only about half the men could sit at one time; the others stood cramped in the aisle or between the seats. Six German guards accompanied us and they had a room in each end of the train. The coach was of the typical 3rd class European style with a number of compartments running down the length of the car, with an aisle along one side. In our little compartment, which could hold six, we had ten men. We took turns standing, sitting, or laying on the floor. The windows were partially painted over, to exclude the view of the civilian population. However, it was possible, by looking through the small open spaces where the paint had flaked off the window, to secure a fairly good picture of the outside.

Our railway coach apparently had the lowest priority on the tracks, since we were usually hooked to the end of a slow freight train. However, it was almost impossible to determine the composition of our train because we were not allowed off the coach, and so we could not see the other railway cars. The trains seemed to travel very slowly, because the tracks had been damaged by bombs every few miles. From Metzlar to Barth is about 600 miles. The trip would take one week, so there was a long ride ahead.

During the first couple of days I attempted to stand by the window as much as possible, to be able to see out. Germany was interesting because of the heavy industrial population, with many small towns, villages and cities. I was also concerned about how the war was going and reasonable deductions could be made from viewing the work habits, dress, war damage, etc.

While on the train, one-fourth of a loaf of bread would be issued to each man daily. A compartment with eight men would receive two complete loaves so each loaf was divided so each man could receive his one-quarter-loaf share. It perhaps should be explained that bread was never wrapped in Europe, and one's first impression of the bread was that it could be mistaken for a short stump of dark wood. In addition, there were never too many sanitary habits and the bread would be stacked on the floor or passed around as if it were a piece of wood. Whenever the train stopped, one or two of the guards would step off the train with two large pails, and secure water. This would then be passed down the train corridor from compartment to compartment.

In addition to the bread we were issued daily, we had our Red Cross parcel. This provided a reasonably ample supply of food. It is in no way compared with an American standard of eating, but we were gradually accepting the facts of life and were adjusting to living with the realities of a country at war.

On board the coach, we had a German interpreter who spoke excellent English. He was a sociable sort of person and had the rank of a sergeant. After a couple of days it was quite obvious to us that he was an officer, but this was just accepted as a way of life to us prisoners by now. He would come over to our compartment and sit and talk for hours.

Our compartment was next to the end and we had the senior Allied officers aboard the train. The senior Allied officer was an Air Force Intelligence Captain, who had asked to go along on one mission to see what it was like and had been shot down. In civilian life he worked for the Bank of America in San Francisco. By sheer coincidence, in our compartment, we also had a British lieutenant who had worked for the Bank of England, and the German sergeant (officer) who was in charge of the train and our interpreter had worked for the German World Bank. These three men had also spent time in the international trade departments of their respective banks. Consequently, there were several people who were known to all three men and a number of international money problems were familiar to all the men. Some of the matters they brought up were wages paid in the various countries, working conditions, what they would do after the war, and banking on the international level in general.

The German interpreter on board apparently had the job of spreading propaganda about the righteous cause of Germany and that we should not hold any bitterness against the Germans. He spoke very freely on all issues and problems. He blamed the war and all problems on the Russians and Jews. I recall asking him what he thought about Hitler. He hesitated a little and said that in five years history would tell if he was good or bad. It was doubtful if he had been assigned to the train to gather information because he was doing most of the talking, and as a matter of fact, we did not know too much.

As we slowly moved through Germany, we had the constant fear of Allied fighter attacks on the train, particularly when we were standing in the large railway yards waiting for another train to pick us up or standing for any other unknown reasons. As we moved through the cities I was greatly surprised by the tremendous amount of damage. It seemed that the cities consisted only of bombed and burned out buildings. This fact did not alleviate my fears, because civilians were always around and by looking at the coach, they could immediately determine it was a prisoner of war railway coach and that they probably held Air Force men.

Some of the cities we passed through were: Kassel, Erfurt, Magdeburg, Leipzig, Wittenburg, Halberstadt, Berlin, Stettin, and Stralsund.

A large number of the rail lines and railway bridges had been bombed out so the train was always changing from one line to another. Germany, incidentally, has a large number of rail lines, so to stop the rail traffic by air attacks alone would be very difficult.

The train trip through Germany took place around the middle of October and the harvest was being completed. The workers were old men and woman and a few children. It was a pathetic sight to see the oxen, old horses or cows pulling the clumsy two and four wheeled carts through the fields. The old men and women, perhaps averaging seventy or so, were following and putting vegetables into the carts. This was almost a scene from another era. It stood out in such sharp contrast to the swift-moving mechanical harvesters in the United States. These memories from my home community lingered in my thoughts.

A most intriguing sight along the railroad were the 88mm gun emplacements. These represented the ultimate in warfare. The gun emplacements usually consisted of four guns mounted on separate turntables. Attempts had been made to camouflage the guns but this was of little value.

If there is anything the Germans were famous for in World War II, it was the 88mm guns. The Krupp Works in Essen had honed these guns to the finesse of a razor with the mechanical marvel of a fine watch. I had seen the results of the 88mm hundreds of times. It was because of one of these guns that I was here. We also saw a number of the 88mm guns placed on flat cars being moved around the country, but staying on the track and firing from the rail car. I'll bet there were some fighter pilots surprised when they cut off to strafe a train and then met an 88mm shell coming at them. They could fire vertically at aircraft or be swing down to the horizontal. These guns were the most dreaded weapon conceived to date by enemy or friend.

Along the railroad we saw hundreds of gangs of workers, busy repairing the road track. In all cases these were foreign workers or captured prisoners of war. I guess a person would call them slave labor. You could tell their status by the German guards standing around while they worked. You could see their clothes; you could see the slow, deliberate movements of a slave, not too fast to get tired and not too slow to be punished.

Injury becomes a problem

It was about at this time that my ankle started swelling and hurting. For a couple of days, at the start of the train ride, I had been standing, and I knew my ankles were a little sore. I assumed they would get better. Now the pain was coming back fast and to my surprise they were swelling. I was therefore given a permanent seat in the compartment. After about 24 hours the ankles got so bad they swelled up as large as my thigh. The interpreter had plenty of aspirin tablets, which I took. There was so much walking back and forth and I had now gone for many days without sleep. My condition seemed to worsen. The guys took turns holding my legs up in the air but it was unsatisfactory. We then struck on an ingenious idea. At the top, on the inside of the coach, was a ledge, so, with the cooperation of all the men, they lifted me to the ceiling of the coach and by using whatever string and straps were available, they tied me to the ceiling of the coach. This helped because I was finally able to get my body into a fully horizontal position and the blood started flowing away from the legs again. I could also sleep up there. Within a day my swelling had gone down and I felt much better.

I vividly recall the first night up on the ceiling ledge in the coach. The train spent the greater part of the night going through Berlin. While we were there, there were several air raids. I would soon learn that the British, flying light, two-engine bombers, were masters at keeping everybody in Germany awake at night. They would fly hundreds of planes at low level in different directions, just causing a general nuisance to the German cities. While slowly moving through Berlin the stark, burned-out buildings seemed to stretch out endlessly in all directions. It just could not seem possible that a city could keep going with all the buildings bombed or burned out.

Life on the train was bearable: however, you can imagine how little personality differences would arise when you are in such cramped quarters. Many of the men would relate some of their experiences with the German population and the events that had occurred between the shoot down and the train ride. The food, besides the German black bread, consisted of a little dried milk, crackers, and one candy bar for the trip, a little instant coffee, and a few other items, which I will describe later.

After leaving Berlin we were headed in a general northeast direction, and headed for a place called Barth, on the Baltic Sea.

Arrival at Stalag Luft I, Barth, Germany

On the morning of the eighth day on the train we arrived at our destination, Stalag Luft I, the largest United States Army Air Force Camp in the world. It held the largest number of officers. Hitler said he was building the German nation to stand for a thousand years, but on the morning I arrived in Barth, I had hopes that the country would collapse in a couple of months. The city of Barth appeared to have a population of about 30,000 persons: the camp itself was located about three miles north of the city, on the edge of the Baltic Sea.

It was a cold, misty morning when we stepped off the train. Again our hair was matted, crawling with lice, our faces unshaven, and we were all very stiff from the long ride. To greet us at the station were a group of perhaps a dozen prison guards and each guard held onto a large, ferocious-looking, black German police dog. These dogs were straining at the end of a short leather leash. The city itself looked old, with all the buildings having been made of brick. Little did I know what was going on within some of the buildings; they looked so old, tired, and innocent. The station was inside the city, so we were forced to march through the town. As we walked, the guards pushed us to move faster. I recall I was going as fast as I could, because, again, my ankles were starting to pain. The streets of the city looked deserted, with only a few old men and women moving around. At the station we did see a few young German Storm Troopers, about 14 or 15 years old. They cast a very cold eye on our group.

As we were called to a halt at the Stalag Luft I main gate I was tired. These last two and a half weeks had been tough. On the outside I looked rough as I walked up to the gate that day. I was still walking with one boot on one foot and a stocking on the right leg. I had no cap or gloves. I was wearing a light blue British woman's army coat that I had been issued in Dulag (temporary POW camp), in Wetzlar, Germany. This woman's coat seemed to be about World War I vintage. For a small girl it was form fitting. The only buttons I could close were the bottom two. The top flapped open in the breeze, and the arms were short and tight. In my hand I carried a little cardboard box that was now empty of food. In looking around at the other American officers, I felt reasonably well dressed, because the others also had an assortment of British, American and German men's and women's clothes. Some limped; some had an assortment of bandages. When looking them over the only impression they would make was that they were a sorry lot of emotionally, physically, and mentally beaten men.

As we stood at the gate I felt a lift of spirits—at last I had come to my home. Perhaps I would be safe, perhaps there would be food, and perhaps there would be a place to sleep, perhaps, perhaps, perhaps....

As the tall gates, constructed of barbed wire, swung open, we were led to a large building, more or less a processing building. Again we filled out some cards, had our picture taken, and received our compound or area assignment. The term compound, in this context, is a group of barracks surrounded by barbed wire and separated from other similar areas. Four of these compounds made up Stalag Luft I.

Then every man took off all his clothes and the clothes were put in a large bag with a tag. The bag was then tossed into a large drum, which revolved over a large fire. This was to delouse the clothing. Then a kerosene can was issued to every man to wash the hairy parts of his body, to supposedly kill the lice, mites, and God knows what.

Then I had my first mass shower, which is, to say the least, an interesting experience. It was not a shower in the commonly understood sense. About 50 guys were crowded into a room and before going in; a small bar of soap was issued to perhaps every sixth man. The water (cold) was turned on for ten seconds. This was all timed like a game to conserve water. Then everybody was supposed to soap up. The guard yelled out something in German and some guy yelled out, "Here comes the water", and it streamed down from the showerheads in the ceiling for another 15 seconds and that was it. Everyone marched out to another large room to secure his clothes. By now the clothes had been deloused, they said. We all had an opportunity to shave, so within half an hour we were in pretty good shape.

After we had completed these processing and cleaning procedures we were moved to our compound. I was assigned to compound number three. By now the word had spread over the entire camp that new "kriegies" (an abbreviation of the German word for Prisoner Of War—Kriegsgefangenen) had arrived, and following the camp construction, we walked down long barbed wire corridors to the far end of the camp. We were moving in single file and as we moved down the barbed wire corridor I had my first look at a real Prisoner of War and I was shocked. They all seemed so pale and thin, many seemed lifeless and seemed little concerned about our coming. They walked slowly, shuffling the sandy soil in front of them with their shoes, their hands in their pockets. The clothing they wore was horrible; their hair was long and cut so funny in various styles. I had never in my life seen human beings like this before. They all seemed to have such high cheekbones; their eyes seemed so sunk in. So many had a strange stare and seemed to express absolutely no emotion about the new prisoners as they passed. As we slowly moved along I would hear someone call out "Hell, Joe. Remember me?", "What shot you down?", "Anybody from the 100th Group?", "When is the war going to end?", "You'll be sorry you ever asked for this assignment", "Why didn't you go to a high class camp?", "Hi, Bill, Remember the night at Smokey Hill?".

As we moved down the thousands of men, the only one I recognized the first time was Lt. Paul Ducharme. It seemed that wherever I would go, he always beat me by a month or two. He had started out living with me at the University of North Dakota. Now he beat me to Stalag Luft I. He had been a glider pilot, and was shot down over France. Soon we were at our compound and another gate opened.

We were, as a group, turned over to the senior Allied officer in the compound, in this case, a guy by the name of Colonel Spicer, with a long handle bar mustache. The Allied officers, U.S. Army Air Force officers, took care of the internal operation of the compound. The colonel took us to a small room and issued us a knife, spoon, bowl, cup, a blanket, and a pillow—that was it. I held all my earthly possessions in my arms and that was all there would be. There were no issues of other things in the months ahead. We were then assigned a barracks or block number and a room number. The colonel then took us to the mess hall and we were each given some barley soup in our bowl, and told to go to our rooms. I was assigned to a room where 15 men were living and I would be number 16. As I walked in with my bowl of barley, they asked me to sit down, which I did. I was now home in prison camp at long last, thank God!

Prisoner Of War Rules. Geneva Convention, 1929

The above title or phrase is used when speaking of the mutual treaty signed at Geneva, Switzerland in 1929. It contains the rules and regulations governing the treatment and care of prisoners of war; of all the signatory powers as of that year, and is binding also on future mutual signators.

The principal clauses governing care and treatment are outlined below:

1. A captured prisoner of war need give only the following information: name, rank and serial number.
2. The food, clothing and shelter shall be equivalent to the army of which he is a prisoner.
3. Medical and spiritual care shall also be equivalent.
4. Prisoners cannot be held in an active combat area.
5. Non-commissioned officers need not do manual work but may be used for supervising enlisted men at work.
6. Officers need not work.
7. Pay shall be equal to pay of men of equal rank in enemy army.
8. Living quarters shall be plainly marked POW.
9. Transportation vehicles shall be plainly marked POW.
10. Solitary confinement will be considered punishment. A prisoner cannot be in solitary more than 30 days or 30 consecutive days for one offense. 3 days must elapse before further solitary can be given.
11. Prisoners will salute men of equal or higher rank.
12. International Red Cross officers will act as inspecting officers.

13. Any questions arising from this treaty will be settled by the International Red Cross in Geneva.

Prisoner Of War life is unique in that it reduces men of all ranks and stations in life to a common denominator. This is, therefore, an experience and activity that few men have an opportunity to participate in during their lifetime.

To live a life, as Prisoner Of War is a dramatic and traumatic experience that none can forget. It is, however, difficult to explain when the day-to-day activities were so dull, monotonous and dreary.

However, it was the experience, when viewed in its overall perspective, that the uniqueness of the episode becomes evident.

Prison life begins

I set the bowl of soup on the little wooden table and the other men took my other belongings and put them on my bed. Then the men immediately gathered around the table where I was about to eat my barley soup.

At this point, an odd incident took place. When I first started eating, there was a little chatter as to where I was from, where I was shot down, how the war was going, etc. I noticed the men were all watching me eat. It seemed as if they expected me to drop the food off the spoon, but then I understood. They were not too interested in me because they were obsessed by the food. All their eyes watched the spoon as I put it in the bowl and took it to my mouth. Their heads and eyes moved in unison as I ate the barley. I thought, are they really Army Air Force officers? As far as food goes, it seemed they had been reduced to the level of animals. I was hungry, but I hoped I would never act like that. Apparently they were receiving a deep down satisfaction from seeing me eat. Soon the barley soup was finished and things returned to normal.

By now it was dark. The other Kriegies helped me make my sack or bed. They all took a little paper or straw out of their mattress and put it in mine. As I lay down in the dark, little did I know that within this room and in similar rooms I would find friendships and comrades who would surpass normal behavior. I don't know what a psychologist would have to say on the subject, but I do know there is something strange and binding among men that hold them together, that makes them think alike when danger threatens. As the going got tougher and rougher, the men became closer and closer. They enjoyed each others company and they formed bonds that were eventually broken only by tears. Women played no part in this life; I was moving into a strange social and cultural structure. It was perhaps as if I was being born again; I was now to find my place in this strange society. I was on my own; no one cared if you were a millionaire or a pauper; nobody cared if you were smart or stupid; nobody cared if you had gone to school or not; nobody cared if you had been promoted or not, nobody cared if you were a Colonel or a 2nd Lt.; nobody cared who you knew or where you came from, nobody cared if you were a hero or a traitor; nobody cared if you were short or tall. They did care about some things: they cared if you were a man, if you would stand beside your buddy, if you were honest, if you were truthful, if you were yourself, perhaps most of all, they cared about you if you cared about them.

Some of the most substantial and meaningful adventures of my life took place at night in the confines of our room. In many ways life is not composed of just food, shelter and clothing. Civilized man lives with a symphony of emotions played against a background of life and death. Many have difficulty in hearing the finely tuned emotions that make life worthwhile.

The room was not too bad. If you have lived and loved in a room, you will always find a place in your heart for that room. The first room I was assigned to had sixteen beds. It measured 15 by 20 feet. The beds were double decked so eight beds took up the space. In a few weeks this complement was increased to 24 men. I noted the kriegies clothes were very dirty and spotted, all the clothes were unpressed. Some clothes had been patched in odd manners because the Kriegies did not have a needle and thread.

As I looked around, many of the men had scars and many had disabled limbs, many were lifeless and strange. This was typical of the prisoners. I was slowly, emotionally, moving into the society of a prisoner of war camp. I liked the feeling of the security I felt with the men. I guess security and the importance of self-ego are the two most important things in a person's life. A thought struck me once in awhile about why women did not seem to play an important part in our life. At this time it seemed strange, but I would soon learn that women did not seem important to the scheme of living. There were various factors at play in this phenomena that, as yet, I did not understand. These will be described at a later point.

I was now starting to live well. I had a great deal more liberty than I had had for three weeks. Every man was a friend, something I had not known for a long time.

The food was poor, but so what. A man could complain but nobody would listen, for we were all in the same boat. That was the life. The only contact we had with the Germans was with the roll call at 8 a.m. in the morning and 5 p.m. in the afternoon. The guards would come around then and close the doors and shutters at 5:30 in the afternoon.

An interesting psychological event would take place at 5:30 as the shutters and doors were locked. We then, instinctively, turned to ourselves. We seemed to move into a world far away from the Germans. I noted the Kriegies stopped visiting between rooms. Anyone who has lived in a dorm at a college knows that at night everyone visits others and everyone ends up in someone else's room. This was not true in prison camp. When the shutters and doors were closed at 5:30, the men sought out their own room. In this room each man found something that cannot be described. As night fell, this was home; here were his friends, his challenges.

Here was a place you could freely express your emotions; here was a place they understood you; here was a place you were appreciated; here were people that were more than friends, these were men who were part of you. You could relax emotionally and physically. No matter what you did in this room, you had from 15 to 23 men who would stand by you. If you lied, they told you; if you thought you were more important than others; they told you; if you were depressed and felt lonely, they carried you. The only situation comparable would be when you were a small child and your mother held you.

In this society it was very important that all men be equal. Any Kriegie who appeared to rise above his friends and buddies was subtly and firmly put back into his social place. That night, as I went to bed, the Kriegies kept talking and discussing things, but I fell asleep. The next thing I knew someone called out "Roll Call". Prison life had begun.

To describing life as a prisoner of war is most difficult because a man's emotions and prejudices became woven into all his thoughts. In the paragraphs and pages that follow, I will attempt to describe to you the life of a Kriegie through his eyes and mind as he wanders and thinks within the barbed wire enclosure.

Normally, men who have been POWs will not necessarily regret their experience, because it represents a type of moral and physical victory never to be forgotten.

It tested man against adversity and against his environment.

There was noise around the room. Someone was shouting "Roll Call". My body seemed welded to the bed. This was the first nights sleep I had had in weeks. As I looked around, I saw some legs falling over bunk beds, then the legs jumped down. I casually asked what to do, and some Lieutenant said to wait for the last call. He said Lt. Smithlien would give it in a couple of minutes. Then I heard the loud voice, last call for Roll Call. That was it. If you were sleeping now, get up and out. Those damn Germans wouldn't wait all day. Out I went with the others. I glanced about quickly and I saw thousands of men lining up in the compound. Each barracks held nearly 250 men. There were ten barracks in the compound. There must be 2500 Air Force officers here.

To me, this was strange, exciting, and perhaps historic. I didn't know but it surely was odd. To the old timers this was a way of life. They knew all the German officers and sergeants who were counting. They knew who could count, who could not count, who would cheat on the count, and would demand a recount. A recall, or recount, is to have all the men brought out and counted over again. We lined up in a normal military formation with four lines, so as the German guard went down the line, he could count by ones and multiply by four. We cooperated with the count to make it fast and accurate.

I guess if you run a prison camp, you just have to count the prisoners and we helped them get it correct most of the time. As a new Kriegie, the first thing I realized was that I was lost and had to look for guidance to the more experienced POWs around me. The old Kriegies seemed to have so much confidence and class. They seemed masters of their emotions and of current conditions.

Off hand, one of the things I first noticed was the way they dressed. They seemed to have a class and style above my level. Yet just a day ago, they seemed like some decrepit creatures. They did not seem to look too bad now. I noted the way they wore the stocking cap; the bars they wore had been hand made; the officer's pink trousers lent an air of style. They were bloused at the ankle of the leg. They used a number of terms that were foreign to me. I could hear them speak of the "Krauts", "picture parade", Pow- wow", "Klim", "North Two", "South One", and hundreds of other terms. These terms would soon be a part of my own vocabulary.

Stalag Luft I was built and organized originally as a British Army and Air Force officers camp and consisted only of about ten barracks and 1500 men. During the early part of the World War II, General Rommel, the German general who led the German Afrika Corps conducted his detailed preliminary training at Barth. At this time, all the prisoners were moved out to other camps. When General Rommel left for Africa, it was again activated as a British Air Force officer's prison camp.

In 1943 the Germans quit sending in British officers to Barth and it was filled with U.S. Air Force officers. The camp eventually grew to about 9,000 men. Incidentally, it was the largest concentration of Air Force officers in the world. American Air Force enlisted men and noncommissioned officers, when captured, were normally sent to prison camps in Poland. To the best of my recollection, the U.S. Air Force seldom sent enlisted men in planes over Europe in combat. I believe it was a policy that only officers and noncommissioned officers were crewmembers and flew in planes in and over Europe in World War II.

Many airmen shot down over Germany just did not make it. There were too many physical and emotional barriers between the time your plane was hit and you arrived at your prison camp. Perhaps 50% were killed in explosions when the planes were hit, or when the planes crashed and 10% died as a result of injuries. A few men, perhaps 5%, became irrational and suffered emotional or mental breakdowns and just disappeared at one of the many stops on the way to the permanent prison camps.

If you had survived the three weeks to a month of train travel, temporary camps, jails, and interrogations, by the time you arrived in the permanent camp you were usually able to take the balance of the ordeal. I was not aware of many Kriegies becoming emotionally or physically sick. If they caused trouble in camp the Germans would usually remove them and that was the last you would ever see or hear of them. A few prisoners in camp were mentally sick, but we all attempted to help them and see to it they did not get into any trouble.

I do not believe that because we were military men we were better able to stand emotional and mental problems. The will and desire to survive play a greater part in one's life then does the military training. Your moral obligation to the military structure drifts away and your instinctive desire to live comes to the foreground, regardless of your morals or training.

Prison organization and structure

The compound, a fenced in section of camp, was about 300 by 300 feet. It was self contained and we did not mix with the other Prisoners Of War in other compounds. An exception was made once and that was on Christmas Eve, when all the prisoners from our compound were allowed to go to the other compound to attend a Christmas Eve program. Very strict security was maintained in this instance. When you were once in a compound the Germans had you and there was no escape. This was a maximum-security prison. Nine hundred and forty methods of escape had been attempted. This Prisoner Of War camp was designed by a genius that knew the mind of a prisoner.

Each barracks was about 85 ft. long and 35 feet wide. Each room held 16 men when I first arrived, but shortly after it was increased to 24 men. The building itself was called a block. Within the block were ten rooms, five on each side. In the end of the building were two small rooms and a nighttime latrine in the other end of the building. The rooms, filled with men, were interesting. It seemed strange, but as I noted earlier, you would go out and visit, but everyone always drifted back to his room, back to his bunk, back to his friends. The rooms were dark, filthy and smoke-filled, but there was a degree of freedom, friendship, and companionship. There were two things Kriegies were all the time; they were hungry and they were cold. These hardships could best be tolerated with your close friends, so they also understood your many moods and emotions better than did the men in the other rooms.

One of the interesting things about a prisoner of war camp is the physical layout of the buildings and barbed wire. In Number South Three Compound, there were ten barracks that held approximately 250 officers each. One small building was set up as a washroom. They did not have individual sinks or basins, but rather a commercial type of washer that activated a stream of water into a large round tub when you pressed down on a lever. Usually each man would wash his face and hands once a day. In another section of the compound there was a latrine. Considered a part of our compound, but separated from it by barbed wire, was a kitchen, a food storage room and a guardhouse.

The compound was surrounded by two 12 foot high barbed wire fences. These two fences were separated by about 10 feet and into this interval the Germans had piles of coils of barbed wire. Then inside the doubled barbed wire there was another six-foot fence. Then twenty feet from the innermost fence of barbed wire there was the infamous "warning wire".

To a Prisoner Of War, the warning wire was the object that stood between himself and freedom. It was a thin steel wire mounted about 18 inches off the ground and was electrified. When anything touched this wire, all hell broke loose. The guards had instructions to shoot to death any object that moved across this warning wire. The physical layout of the guard towers made this warning wire lie directly in the line of sight and the line of fire of all the guns.

At night the searchlights kept slowly moving around the camp, but much of the time they concentrated on the warning wire. Anything beyond this wire was beyond debate or contention. Over that wire there would be no more questions. No further orders or shouts or human life for that matter. This was the forbidden world we had left but hoped to return to some day. Inside the warning wire we could play our tricks, live our life as best we could, silently fighting the Germans in our subtle manners, but at the warning wire all horseplay stopped. Here was a line that no man had ever crossed; yet it looked so simple to the eye of the uninformed. On a few occasions an officer would test the German system by raising a foot towards the wire but at once the rifles were raised, and the searchlight would come on, and the sirens would start screaming.

The beds occupied an important part of Kriegie life and each Kriegie attempted to make his bed as comfortable and as homey as possible with the equipment and tools at hand. In one of the rooms I lived with 23 other Kriegies. We slept on shelves next to one another and we had no room for fixing, adjusting, or making ourselves more comfortable. The so-called German mattress, issued to a Prisoner Of War, was but a shallow sack with a little straw, paper, or excelsior. Anyone who has spent a winter on a wad of shredded paper will appreciate the misery.

When I slept on the shelves, I was stuck and could do nothing to better myself. I just slept on the loose fitting boards and learned to sleep by growing cold and numb.

When I moved into a four-man room, a great event came to pass. The Germans issued the mattress filler in bales which were tied together with baling wire and I, as Executive Officer, had been placed in charge of issuing this shredded paper or other filler to the new Kriegies so they could make a mattress.

I confiscated all the wire, perhaps about 20 feet, but this was enough so that I could weave myself a sack that would fit my size and be the perfect Kriegie-bed.

So, as soon as I could, I rolled up the wire and disappeared into my room. Then I began the reconstruction of my bed. I asked the other officers if they wanted any wire and they said no, saying they would sooner have a couple of my boards to make their beds more even. I took out the few boards and distributed these among the other men in the room. Then I used the wire and constructed a bed that would sag in the middle and more closely conform to my body as I lay in a spoon fashion, all curled up. My rank and position in Kriegie camp had finally paid off. I had been in a position where I could get the wire and then go ahead and construct this bed that, in many ways, resembled a hammock. That night I slept in a comfortable bed compared to what I had been using.

During the winter months, one of the most uncomfortable aspects of our living was the cold rooms. The little coal we had was never used for heating. It was used to heat food. If it had been used to raise the temperature in the room a few degrees it would have compounded the winter problems.

The problem was that with 24 men in the small room, the humidity from their breath was nearly 100%. This vapor was continually condensing on the ceiling, walls, windows, clothes and other objects to form frost. On the ceiling the frost was half an inch thick and during the day, as the temperature rose from a little cooking we did, the water would drip down on the floor and beds. What was really miserable was that many times your outer clothing and blankets would turn stiff at night from the frozen moisture. It was not a question of keeping warm; the problem resolved itself to keep from getting too cold. To be dry and cold is not too bad, but being wet and cold is really miserable. I noticed that my legs would grow numb first, but my arms and hands I could wrap around myself to keep them warm.

There were a few men who had wristwatches, perhaps one out of twenty-five. Most of the prisoners had lost their watches along the way to camp. Many of the men had carried military watches and the Germans confiscated these. There were no pocketknives in camp because these were considered to be cold weapons. One of the personal items the Germans issued to each man when he arrived in camp was a small block of tooth cleaner. This block of tooth cleaner measured about an inch square and one-fourth inch thick. It was hard. To use it you dipped your toothbrush in water and then rubbed it on this block, picking up a little of the cleaner on the bristles. A block of this cleaner would last a year. The toothbrush the Kriegie owned was received from the Red Cross when he arrived in camp.

A Kriegie would normally never carry anything in his pockets. Perhaps if he smoked he would carry a package of cigarettes in his shirt pocket, but no matches. Matches were a luxury item and fire was carried from room to room and men smoked in turn to keep a cigarette fire going. This, however, was in no way a hardship, just a little inconvenient. The Germans issued a small book of matches to each room once a month. German matches were of very poor quality. The wood in the match was thinner than a cheap toothpick, which meant that to light the match you would have to hold the match head close to the striking surface and strike it very carefully or the head would break off and be lost.

Military rank did play a part in the life of Americans in Prisoner Of War camps. It would be hard to conceive of a large group of men numbering several thousand, living together without some type of organization. If the men were military, the resulting organization would be called a military organization, regardless of how it was organized. The structure of the unit would be based on echelon of responsibility and authority. The designated men would automatically use rank as a symbol of position. Similarly, all large units such as colleges or manufacturing companies must have the same basic organizational structure in order to function.

The above paragraph is mentioned, because technically, when you were captured and became a POW, you were treated the same as all other men. This is true, but to the treated equally, you must have some sort of discipline and organization, so the lowest ranking man in a camp will receive his fair share of a ration of food. It was also imperative that the German authorities have someone in authority to discuss problems with, such as roll call, disease, camp rules and regulations, distribution of rations, clothing and housing problems.

Kriegie rooms were very sparse. There were no pictures, no drawings, map, mirrors, clocks, or other decorative objects on the wall. However, beside each bed, each Kriegie had nailed or hung an empty Red Cross box wherein he put his personal items. The nails used for the box were pulled out of the barracks wall by using a couple of table knives and a little ingenuity. The table knife and spoon issued by the Germans were used for many unintended purposes. Many Kriegies made maps, but placing them on the wall usually led to their confiscation when the German ferrets came around at night for the picture parade or recount by rooms.

Each Kriegie room also had a table similar to a backyard picnic table or an army mess hall table. This table never had any objects on it except when we were eating. The POWs used the table for playing cards, reading books, or just for sitting and talking.

The room, however, was not bare in appearance. If you were to walk into a Kriegie room, the following impressions would strike you: it is dark, it's very cluttered, it's very crowded—with two or three-decked bunks staring at you, regardless of which way you turned. Many persons would be talking, and a number of small activities would be going on simultaneously. Nothing would seem organized. Men would be wearing all kinds of clothing and would be in all states of dress. As you kept observing, you would begin to detect various common centers of interest.

Each man had his bed in this room, or what you would better describe as a den. It, the bed, was small, dark, and rather hidden in the room. The bed had a four-inch sideboard and a half-inch mattress, which made it more like a shallow box than a bed. The small wall space around the beds would be covered with small Red Cross boxes, which had been nailed to the wall.

In one corner would be a bleak stove with a black stovepipe going up through the ceiling. Around the stove would be more cupboards made from Red Cross boxes nailed to the wall. On the floor near the stove would be a small German broom. The brooms were made by the Kriegies from long grass the Germans would issue the camp from time to time. The grass would be cleaned and fashioned into a small bundle about two feet long and tied at the top with some of the strands of grass. Next to the stove there would also be a small pail holding the small coat ration when it was issued. This was usually empty.

Each man had all his clothing either on his body or on the bed so there would be no clothing hanging up around the room. If you didn't wear it, you slept on it.

To add to the bleakness, I can never recall seeing a building or any object painted. There were no painted objects in the room, nor were there any painted objects in camp. When the buildings in camp were new, they were a light tan in color, but at the end of a year, they had taken on a dull grey appearance that tended to blend with the color of the soil in the camp at Barth.

Prison food

Based on the number of men in a block or barracks, the Germans would usually make a ration issue of some type of food to the block or barracks each day. The ration officer, who had been appointed by the block commander, would report to the German Supply Building each morning at 9 a.m. and would draw his rations for his block for the day. The Germans knew the number of men in each block and this would be the basis for the issue. For example, one briquette of coal would usually be issued each day to each man. Therefore, in an average barracks, 250 officers would get 250 lumps of coal. If the issue for the day included potatoes, then perhaps 125 potatoes would be issued, if the issue were one-half potato per man per day. Some days there would be black bread, say two slices per man. You would rapidly compute in your head, 500 slices, and if there were 25 slices in a loaf, then 20 loaves of bread. The above three items were usually issued each day.

The Germans themselves would not divide the food; they would determine a proportionate share for each compound. If, for example, there were 2,000 men in each of four compounds, then whatever came in would be split four ways, and it would be up to the senior Allied officer in each compound to do the actual dividing. It should be remembered nearly 9,000 officers were in the camp and food was an important element in all activities. A person could be thankful if he received anything. When the rations became so slim they were not worth dividing. For example, how would you divide 10 bushels of potatoes, a dozen loaves of bread, a pail of alfalfa, a dozen cabbages, and a pail of carrots, among 10,000 men? The answer was to make soup, and then divide the soup. The making of the soup and dividing of the soup was taken care of by the U.S. officers and divided by the officers.

One who has been a prisoner of war can say that one has not lived until one has had to divide a couple of pails of soup among 250 starving men. Only officers with a character beyond reproach would be selected as ration officers. One had to be strong, like an umpire in a ball game, making decisions and suffering the tirades of fellow officers, who, if they thought they had been cheated out of a spoon full of soup, would not be afraid to voice their opinion as to your ability, character, and brains. This was a part of Kriegie life accepted by everyone.

The Red Cross box was the key link between starvation and life to the POW in Germany. It was well put together as far as foodstuffs were concerned, and contained a number of items. However, there were always things missing which a person would want. Some of the items which I would have liked to have seen put in each parcel were a paper back book on any subject, a small scissors in some of the boxes, however, this would be considered a "cold weapon" and confiscated before it reached the prisoner A needle and thread would have been handy, pencil and paper would have been a good morale booster, a dictionary would have been nice, a few items like band aids or other first aid supplies would have been valuable. Vitamins would have played an important part in keeping the prisoners in good health.

The Red Cross is a fine, large, considerate organization. There are many valuable service organizations, which contact service men from time to time, however, head and shoulders above all of these social organizations stand the Red Cross. When the going gets tough in war or peace, the Red Cross is the only unit that can function effectively. Its service is many times restricted by the complications of war or catastrophe, but it does have the ability, resources, and organization, to do more than all the other organizations put together.

From time to time you may hear the fact that the Red Cross charged money for a cup of coffee, while some other organization gave the men free coffee. I cannot attest to the truth of the above statement, but to compare the Red Cross with any other service organization is doing a great disservice to the Red Cross. When the need is the greatest, such as a POW camp, the Red Cross rises above all other humanitarian units and, in many cases, means the difference between life and death to men in some of the most remote corners of the world.

Part of our food supply was sent to us through the International Red Cross. The parcels would first be shipped to Geneva, then by train to Barth, Germany. From Barth they would go by charcoal burning trucks to an anti-aircraft school located about half a mile from the camp. From the school warehouse, the parcels would be hauled by horse drawn wagons to a building in the compound. Here the Germans would open the parcels, confiscate a small packet of pepper, and then, with an axe, they chopped a large hole in the top of every can. The reason the pepper was taken out was because the Kriegies in throwing in the eyes of the dogs in an escape attempt could use it. The cans of food were cut so that none of the canned goods could be stored and thereby used in escape and evasion. Following the above ritual, the number of parcels would be determined and that number divided into the number of prisoners in the compound. Usually there would be one parcel for four men or perhaps one parcel for six men. The further breakdown into rooms would be made by the block rations officer.

The Red Cross parcels were intriguing in their make up. Some of the items contained were a small package of cheese, small jar of instant coffee, a can of dried milk, a quarter pound of sugar, a small box of crackers, a packet of salt, one can of spam, six packages of cigarettes, and one D Bar. The D Bar was the most important item in the box and it represented a medium of exchange for all Prisoners Of War. The number of D Bars he could accumulate measured a man's wealth and economic power within the camp.

The D Bar received it's name from the fact that it was a chocolate bar about 3 inches long and ¾ inch thick and packaged by the government in brown wrapping paper. It was part of the Army prepackaged ration known as type D. The chocolate was excellent in quality and contained about as much candy as a large Hershey chocolate bar. Cigarettes also were a medium of exchange. However, I noted that the D-Bar had a more basic value and, to a certain extent, formed the basis for other types of exchange being used.

Under normal conditions, a D-Bar was the equivalent of a carton of cigarettes. In dealings between Kriegies, the cigarette packages represent the fractional money and the D Bar the standard. For example, if a Kriegie wanted to buy a home made set of Air Force insignia pilot wings, he perhaps would have to pay 2 D Bars and 5 packages of cigarettes. A can of dried milk would sometimes sell for one and a half D Bars and at other times, perhaps 2 D Bars. With D Bars you could buy clothes, insignia, food, cigarettes, matches, paper, in fact, anything of value had a D Bar value. Many Kriegies would buy and sell food with the idea in mind that they could increase their D Bar fund or make money. The fact that we had no money was of no interest. If we had had money, coins or currency, it would have been worthless. As in a normal economy, some of the Kriegies would be broke and some would have a dozen D Bars.

It would come to mind that with so many D Bars floating around perhaps someone would steal from other Kriegies. There was never any stealing from one another. When you have 10,000 hungry men, no law or rules need be stated or discussed as to what would have happened to an officer who had stolen a D Bar. He would have been swiftly, silently, and surely found in the morning, lying still in the outdoor latrine.

There are hundreds of unwritten rules and codes of conduct among a group of men. It would be an interesting study in psychology to attempt to understand the deep rapport established between groups of men being held prisoner of war. I think every Kriegie felt a tremendous sense of security with other Kriegies. Here was a classic case of "one for all, all for one". There was a deep sense of equality among the men. They were all officers and had various ranks, but above all they were Prisoners Of War and all faced the same problem of life and death. There was no such thing as one man being better than another man.

When life is reduced to its essentials, men start thinking; reasoning, talking, acting, and becoming more and more like each another. Another reason for the close feeling between the Kriegies was, since they were all in exactly the same position, there was no envy, jealousy, or status distinction. These are factors, which in a normal society, lead to underlying problems of struggle and desires that tend to infringe on other people and their rights and possessions.

Klim, a symbol of food

The Borden Milk Company may never know the Klim can was a symbol of Kriegie life in World War II. It contained about a pint measure of dried milk. Using this simple can, the prisoners mixed the contents with water to make whole milk. When the can was empty it was used for many purposes, some of which are: the lead in the seam was melted and used to make officer insignia, it was cut up and made into pots and pans, attached to the end of a stick it was used as a stomper to wash clothes, it was used to build air pipes in escape tunnels, it was used as a shovel to dig tunnels, it was used as a bowl or a cup, and lastly, its name Klim, milk spelled backwards, was applied to many items of manufacture and to a Kriegie it still means something I cannot describe.

In accordance with the rules of war, a prisoner is supposed to receive the same ration as that given to the enemy's own army. This, of course, is not done. I do believe the Germans made a reasonable attempt to give us what was available or, in reality, what was left. The principal issue was made almost daily and would be one lump of coal per Kriegie, half a potato, a small portion of cabbage, then, once a week, each prisoner would get half a turnip, a little artificial butter, and on a couple of occasions we received a slice of cheese, a little sugar, salt and about once a month we would receive horse meat soup.

On two occasions we received an issue of horsemeat of about one eighth pound per man. The horsemeat tasted good. However, we were advised that these were horses that had been killed in the war or died on nearby farms and then hauled into the camp. Much of the flesh had been rotted by the time it came to the camp, but the Germans, in cooperation with some of the Kriegies would cut up that which could be eaten and a fair division was made.

The biggest trouble with the meat would be the maggots, but maggots were a part of Kriegie life. When we received soup it seemed that often maggots would be in the soup. When I think of maggots, I always think of the most wonderful food in the world; this was barley soup. This was a dish that all the Kriegies lived for, and we usually received it once every two weeks. I don't know why, but I know of no other food that can lift the body and spirits higher than barley soup. Through our little underground, we would know about three days in advance when the Germans were going to issue barley soup and all life then would point to this moment when the bowl of soup was set before you. Then everything in life seemed worthwhile.

In the soup, and especially in the barley soup, it seemed there would always be maggots, but the cooked maggots were exactly the same color as the cooked barley. Most of the Kriegies did not look too close because the maggots did not spoil that delicious taste that bordered on ecstasy. The maggots were, of course, all dead, and I guess they had some food value.

In thinking of the artificial butter that was issued, it was really a white substance that looked like oleomargarine. It was made from coal and had no food value. Sometimes, when we received a pound of it, we would use it to spread on the coal briquettes to gain more heat for our fire for cooking.

Cooking and preparation of food amongst the Prisoners Of War was a science and an art. There were various types of organizational structures and schemes arranged to gain the most from the food at hand. In the first room I lived with 16 men. There the food was put into a pool and then there were two officers voted in as cooks. These cooks then had all the Red Cross parcels. German rations and coal were added, and from these elements they made the food. Only two meals, or perhaps it would be better said that we ate twice a day, once after roll call in the morning, and then our supper after roll call in the evening. In eating or preparing food, one of the first things would be to secure the pots and pans in which to cook the food. These had to be constructed by the Kriegies themselves. A basic cooking utensil was the deep and shallow pans made from tin cans.

The stove provided by the Germans left many things to be desired. The stove would be properly described as a tile heating stove. This is a stove designed, not for throwing out heat in the sense we use stoves in the United States. Their stove reminded me of one of the old charcoal burner used about the turn of the century in the United States. It was approximately 18 to 24 inches square and about 3 ½ feet high. The walls were made of tile brick and faced on the outside with a brown colored tile. The top was a smooth tile surface. So the first thing a Kriegie would do was to tear off the top and make a tin lid to fit over the top. Then the system providing a draft would be increased so that a fire of any degree temperature could be produced. After the stove had been modified, it worked reasonably well. The stove was used only to cook food, never used for heating, because we never had enough coal.

In the preparation of food perhaps the most essential item would be the cooking of the potatoes, cabbage, rutabaga, and heating of water for coffee. These items were cooked or prepared on a rather communal basis. Normally, late at night, each man would often have some small personal item to eat that he had saved. The ultimate in night food preparation would be a small piece of coal for the stove, a piece of black bread, a little cheese and a little sugar or jam. With these you could make the most delicious toasted cheese sandwich. Under normal conditions, you could have this about once every two weeks and it was a special treat.

After the preparation of the German rations, they would be cooked and then equally divided into all the Kriegie's bowls. One of the arts would be that of dividing the food. Usually the divider would be a Kriegie for whom you had both respect and admiration. After the food was divided, there was no mention of one man receiving more than another. This, again, was one of the unwritten laws.

In some rooms with 24 or 25 men, it became unwieldy to consolidate the food and then the group would be divided into smaller groups of four to eight men who would operate their own food service scheme. This worked reasonably well as they would usually have to take turns eating at the table and using the stove. It worked out better than one would imagine.

It should be remembered the only dishes a man had were a bowl, cup, knife, and spoon. If you lost or broke one, that was it—there was no further issue, and you would have to use a can.

Food had a direct bearing on all the conversation and what a person would be thinking about. For example, during times of ample food the conversation would cover all topics from the Air Force, planes, work, school, religion, Kriegie stories, automobiles, Germans, when the war would end, etc. As the food supply grew low, the topics of conversation gradually drifted to food. When only a couple of slices of black bread were issued each day, the conversation would be dominated by food. The men would discuss what they liked to eat, what they would eat on their first meal in the States, that they would go into the restaurant business following the war, when the next Red Cross parcel would arrive, and the latest rumor concerning the issue of barley soup by the Germans. They would talk about food 18 hours a day and still go to sleep hungry.

During one of the low food periods I saw one of the most degrading acts. Although it was normal and human, it was strange to see the event take place.

The German mess hall, which faced against a section of our compound, had a large window out of which the Germans threw their kitchen slop every day at about noon. At that time, after finishing peeling their potatoes, the officers would crowd around this window, waiting for the slop or garbage to be thrown out. Then, at the given moment, the guard would throw a large pail of slop, which included a lot of potato peelings, out the window. Many officers would be hit while the others would dive to the ground and fight over the peelings. After a mad scramble the officers would leave the area, clutching three or four peelings or small potatoes, which they would take back to their room and make into a soup.

In one of the rooms in which I lived during a prolonged food shortage, I had been voted to go to the German kitchen to receive the daily ration of soup. When I left the room at the call of the Compound Ration Officer, I would take with me a little pail. The men in the room would wish me good luck. When I returned to the room, the POWs would crowd around the door and, with anxious eyes, would peer into the pail. Some days, when the pail was fuller, they were happy. Some days, when the pail was nearly empty, the faces were sad. The pail would be set on the table and it would be constantly stirred as it was divided equally. Following the meal we would hurry and lie down and keep that little full feeling for as long as possible. It would last perhaps 15 minutes to half an hour and then the craving for food would return to our bodies.

During periods of low food, one of the interesting psychological facts would be the dreams one would have. Every night one would dream of eating. It is just like being thirsty. If a person is really thirsty he will dream he is drinking water during periods of the night, yet you never get a full, satisfied feeling. When you are hungry, you dream of eating and you constantly eat but you are never satisfied. I can recall dreaming of eating bushels of cream puffs but being unable to satisfy the hungry feeling that would never leave me. I woke up in the morning feeling odd and depressed.

The Germans also had a rough time during the latter part of the war. The food was poor and cigarettes, coffee, soap, and many other essentials of life were almost non-existent. As a nation, the people lived very poorly. Every ounce of effort and food went into the war effort.

The German officers lived very well. They lived in luxury compared to the German enlisted men. Many of the officers were of the upper level in the German culture. They were well decorated, wore beautiful conservative uniforms, wore monocles, used canes, and many had Heidelberg scars from the professional academic community. These were the scars they had cut into their cheeks below the eyes. The scars were an act and status symbol of military discipline, honor, and courage. They formed a visible bond among the German elite military community.

A couple of weeks before the war ended, we noted we again received Red Cross parcels. These had long been forgotten in the winter months, and we were on a steady diet of German Army leftovers. We were told by our senior Air Force officers these Red Cross parcels had been stored in Lübeck, Germany, a city about fifty miles from Barth on the Baltic. Further, he said, the German commander of the camp had gone to the port city and demanded or ordered the parcels be shipped to the camp because he did not want to be caught with starving men on his hands. The German camp commander also rounded up some potatoes so that the last week of the war we were eating a reasonable Kriegie diet.

During my stay in camp, on two or three occasions, we were issued German cigarettes. These were exceptionally poor and we gave them back to the German officers and guards as a matter of fact, rather than as a bribe or treat. On one occasion, near Christmas, we received beer, but this was but foaming water and had little food value or taste. At Christmas in 1944 the Red Cross issued each of us a pipe and two cans of Prince Albert smoking tobacco.

In the art of manufacturing items in camp the Kriegies were ingenious, to say the least. One of the basic items would be the pan, made from a number of tin cans. This pan was used for cooking, frying, baking, heating water, or what have you. The procedure in making a pan was to take about 10 cans and cut them into smooth flat rectangular sheets of tin. The sheet was cut and trimmed by a table knife. This knife had a hole in the end, which was held by a nail in the crack of the table. By placing the tin on the table, the knife would close down, cutting the metal to the required dimensions. Following the preparation of the flat pieces of tin, the metal was scored twice along the edge and a double fold was made along the long edge. When two of these pieces of tin had been loosely folded, they were slid together and laid on a flat surface and pounded flat. Gradually additional pieces of tin were added until a surface about 18 inches square had been formed. Then it was a relatively easy procedure to fold up the sides and ends and double fold the tops to form a smooth edge. As food was prepared in the pan, the cracks soon sealed themselves with food matter to form a watertight container. These were made in sizes and styles limited only by the Kriegie's imagination and determination.

Another item manufactured requiring skill and care was the cigarette pack holder. This was constructed by cutting about 40 strips of tin a quarter of an inch wide and about twelve inches long. These strips were then woven together to form a box in the shape of a cigarette package. They made covers, springs, and hinges to make them highly sophisticated and desirable. One item used a great deal was the razor blade sharpener. This was made by cutting a leather strip off the top of the shoe and then wrapping this strip around a small round piece of wood about the size of an empty spool of thread. To this was attached a handle to make it turn and the device was placed on a little stand. Then, by holding the razor blade in the hand and turning the leather spool, one could do a reasonable job of sharpening the razor. Spoons were cut out of wood; tin cans formed the basic material for a number of household items.

A Kriegie's life is wrapped around food at all times. He sleeps, dreams, thinks, and talks about food. Despite the fact that food was scarce in camp, the little we had was utilized in many ways because the Kriegies loved to work with food. A good test of a real Kriegie was to ask him if he would rather spend a night sleeping with a movie star or have a good meal. A good meal was, of course, always the answer. If he said he would rather sleep with a movie star we knew he was lying to himself and lying to us. To the average Kriegie, the above question was stupid because everybody knows that food is much more enjoyable than a woman. No one ever asked what the second choice would be because we were again talking about food, the most enjoyable thing in the world.

Psychologically, the conversation about food dominated the daytime hours and it would dominate a person's dreams. I had the same dreams many times. It was where I was sitting at home eating and after finishing everything on the plate, I was still hungry. I would ask for a second helping but I was always uncomfortable or embarrassed that I would put too much food on the second helping. I would eat it and still feel hungry and very frustrated because I had my strange hungry feeling. As the other folks left the table I would also, but I always felt they just did not understand my strange feeling. I had no knowledge as to why I was still hungry. I just prayed it would not be too long until I had another meal.

During the latter part of the war my mind became a little warped in regards to food because I would daydream about food and my thoughts were always about the same. This thinking was wrong, but there was nothing I could do about it. These thoughts, in the daytime, followed a well-set pattern and my thoughts drifted along with no effort on my part. This fantasy took place at home. I knew I would be home for a while following liberation and then I would eat and eat and eat. I would have breakfast with Edwina and her folks and then I would take off for my folk's home and they would invite me to eat breakfast. I would tell them I had not eaten. Following this breakfast I would go to the local café and order breakfast. Then I would go back to my in-laws home and have a lunch, always eating heartily, then to my folks, and then to the restaurant. This would occupy my entire day and I thought of many excuses in case they should find out about my excessive eating. They would just never understand my feelings and me. These thoughts would float through my mind several times a day, with my thinking going into very specific items. In my mind, I could see the actual food on the plate.

In prison camp, salt was number one on our food list. For several months we did not have salt and it became an important topic of conversation. I recall when I wrote home to Edwina; salt was the first thing on my list of things that I wanted. We all maintained the lack of salt makes a person very weak. Whether this is real medically or a psychological problem, I do not know. We all blamed it on the lack of salt and I recall the men so often talking about the fact when they got back to the states the first thing they would eat would be a slice of bread and butter covered with a thick layer of salt. When things get real tough and food runs out, salt is missed more than any other item of food. The others are nice to have, but we all felt we had to have salt to keep going. What tobacco or cigarettes are to a smoker, salt is to the eater.

On certain occasions the Kriegies made special food dishes. One of the most popular was a cake made in the following fashion. Grate up a cup of soda crackers, one half cup of powdered milk, a tablespoon of oleo margarine, half a cup of sugar, a cup of water, half a cup of raisins, and a cup of black bread crumbs. This was then all mixed up and put in a shallow pan on top of the stove and baked for half an hour. Not only was it very delicious but very filling and really gave a person a good feeling for a long time. The cake was cut up into squares and each person received his share.

In my mind I can clearly see Captain Blackburn, one foot up on the bench by the table, grating crackers with a homemade grater. As he was grating and arguing with his fellow POWs, he would not be looking at what he was doing and the ends of his fingers would be cut when the cracker became too short. He would let out a couple of curse words and add that a little blood would make the better cake. Then I can see Ainsworth stirring the mixture on the stove, getting free advice from his roommates—he was stirring too slow, or too fast, and arguing with someone over the relative merits of Texas A&M College. Throughout the cooking procedure there would be an air of good feeling and happiness in the room because we would soon have something good to eat.

We also made delicious pudding using the same ingredients as in the above cake, except you added about twice as much water, and cooked it for five minutes on top of the stove. You did not have to cook it, but if you had the extra lumps of coal to cook with, it tasted better. It too was divided with a precision known only to a POW cook of starving men.

On the few occasions when we received a can of Spam we would cut it up into tiny cubes and mix with potatoes that had been cut real small. We cooked these two items together and when the potatoes had boiled we stirred it all up and had a delicious Spam and potato mixture. This I would say would be the top in food.

Whenever we did have meat, we usually saved some and made meat gravy. We ground it up and mixed it with powdered milk and water. This was poured over the mashed potatoes. The potatoes were always mashed with a wooden club after cooking because it would have been impossible to divide them equally if they were in their original round shape.

One thing that was very good was to take black bread and first slice it real thin and then slice it again crossways, thereby making small cubes. We then roasted these on the stove and used them as breakfast food by pouring mixed powdered milk over the roasted cubes of bread. It tasted exactly like Grape Nuts, if not a little better.

On two or three occasions we made wonderful dessert called Prune Whip. First you take a small box or two cups of prunes and carefully shaved off the meat, then the prune meat would be cut into small pieces. Next you took the stones and cooked them over the stove to remove the last traces of the prune meat. This water was then mixed with powdered milk and sugar and then more water was added and then the prune meat would be added and the whole thing boiled in a Kriegie pan over the stove for 10 minutes. Following the boiling, it was cooled. Then we mixed it up and as we mixed it, it took in some air, the result being a greater volume than when we had started. This was really good and I remember we made this for dessert on Christmas Eve as a real celebration treat.

After eating the prune whip, the stones were opened up and you ate the meat inside the stones. This was also very good.

Normally when food got short, the best way to stretch it is to make soup. On some occasions I recall we stretched food almost to the breaking point. If we were issued one potato for four men a discussion would ensue as to how best to use it. The scheme we usually used worked well. We took the potato and sliced it real thin, making perhaps 25 slices out of one medium potato and then we boiled the slices in two quarts of water. After this had boiled we divided the soup four ways. As you divided the soup, you continually stirred so everyone got the same amount of solid matter. These little tricks and procedures became a part of your life after a few weeks in the camp.

In the German bread which was issued, it was assumed by all that a large part of the bread was erzats, meaning it was filled with substitute items of no food value. In the bread it was said that saw dust had been processed and added to the bread as a filler. This was a fairly common technique used by the Germans to stretch the available food. It apparently was used extensively in sausage, pastry, bread, candy, soup and other common items of food. Whatever ingredients were added, they were fillers and did not add or detract from the good taste of the food. The "Wheels", the Air Force higher officials, were always warning us that ground glass had been found in the bread. I never looked too close and never noticed any.

Long dark nights

At 5:30 in the afternoon the door on the blocks were locked with a chain and lock on the outside. Now life as known to few men started inside the rooms. In the fall and summer it was still light inside, but during the winter it was dark and the officers would drift to their own rooms. There was a small light in the ceiling of each room that helped, if the electricity was on. At about nine o'clock the Krauts would blink the lights a couple of times and then a couple of minutes later they would go out. It was immaterial if you had light or did not have light. If you could not do what required light in the day light hours, there was something wrong. There would be a few Kriegies playing cards when the lights went out and they would let out a few curse words when it went black, but so what. If he should have played the ace instead of the duce, he could try tomorrow.

When the lights went out the Kriegies moved into a strange, emotional world. Now they were alone. Everything seemed so far away. Now a rapport was established between all the men that cannot be explained. There were from 15 to 25 men in a small room. Once in a while an officer would probe the climate to attempt to make him more important than the other men. The ego was still at work. After a moment of silence there would be a stabbing remark made that would cut him down to his real size and he himself and we would have no more trouble. In fact, if any officer cared to test the strength of 24 men he was more than welcome. There would be one less for breakfast in the morning and he knew it. P.S. And no red tape or tears. Death is silent.

In the evening, after it was dark, we usually had a program. I noted this worked extremely well. There would be no special POWs who would act as program director or announcer, but we drifted into an informal program. These 24 officers represented an interesting cross section of life. In one of my rooms, one was a Greyhound bus driver, one was a gold miner, one was the son of a Hollywood insurance executive, one farmed in Wyoming, some came from poor families, some from rich families. All had been crewmembers in the United States Army Air Corps and all had been shot down. One way or another all had become prisoners. All had gone to different colleges and training camps. Some had been drafted and some had volunteered. A couple had graduated from Military Schools. Some had been in trouble, some were married, and some were single. All had many experiences and all had some special knowledge and all were interesting.

During the evening there would usually be one officer who would sing a Kriegie song or two. Then some officer would relate some experience in his being shot down and captured. There would always be two or three jokes, a few riddles, and a few stories about women these men had run into and visited in life. Some would relate experiences at home, events, which took place in the Army or perhaps in college, long discussions about how the war was going, and individual officers would relate their hard and long bombing missions. There would always be discussion about what they were going to do after the war. These programs would last from two to four hours and all the Kriegies would participate and relate interesting events.

Lt. Ole Olson from Zumbrota, Minnesota would discuss an event that happened while driving a Greyhound bus between Chicago and Minneapolis. Lt. Ray from Tennessee told of his law school days and how he had given a dissertation on how to raise champion bird dogs. Interspersed in the program would be requests for a song by one or more of the talented singers. I recall in our room we had one professional entertainer who would sing the solos. Certain Kriegies were particularly adept at telling jokes and they would always be called on to give a couple each evening. One of these was Lt. Siltimake from Wyoming. There was a concerted effort to keep the discussion or program moving so it would be of interest to all the men. The programs were conducted in a relaxed atmosphere. During the program there might be a couple of air raids but the Allies had never bombed our camp so we felt reasonably safe. Because the nights were usually still and clear, we could usually hear the ack-ack and the few German fighters go up after the formations. Despite the outside activity, programs in the room would continue until about two o'clock in the morning.

Kriegies are perpetually hungry. I guess the average Kriegie lost about 40 to 50 pounds in camp. When I arrived I was at about 160 and the day I left I was down to about 120. However, this loss occurred over a period of about nine months, so there was no sudden drop. Despite the loss of weight, I would say the health of all the men remained very good. The loss of weight does affect a person in odd ways. For example, during the winter a person would freeze a great deal more because he had no fat on his body. We stood during the long roll calls outside when the temperature was around zero without overshoes. Your feet almost froze to the ground. Mine never froze, but twice a day roll calls soon caused them to hurt and pain all the time in the winter months. The most miserable thing about being thin was a prisoner must always sleep on his side. The reason for this was with no heat in the building and the outside temperature at zero, the inside of the room became covered with frost and all your clothing, blankets, and such became soggy, wet, and frozen stiff. In order to conserve heat, the only way you could do so was to curl up and pull one's knees up as close to the head as possible. This inevitably resulted in your hip resting on a cold, hard surface and it would grow numb and gradually the numbness would move down the legs. When the morning came and you started moving the numbness would leave the legs. Your body had so little flesh it was your bones resting on the bed. Your hips were constantly sore.

An interesting academic question would be how would 10,000 women act under similar conditions? Would it be possible for 25 women, for example, to live in a room that would be about 16 x 20 feet? Man can do it. However, it does take cooperation from all the men. I can never recall one Kriegie striking another Kriegie. There were some heated arguments over such things as: "Was the P-47 better than the P-51 Mustang fighter? Were the Wright Cyclone engines better than the Pratt and Whitney? Would the war end in one month or three months, etc? These obviously did not cut into anyone's emotions or feelings unless it was 3 o'clock in the morning and the rest of the room had heard enough. Someone would voice his opinion that it was time to go to sleep and the argument would stop. The feeling was they could start it in the morning and at least they would not bother everyone.

As I have mentioned, part of the time in camp was spent in relating combat experiences to one another. Some of the guys really had terrific experiences, both in the air and on the ground. I recall one officer who was flying as a co-pilot on a B-17 when it was hit directly in the bomb bay by anti aircraft fire and the ship exploded. He was knocked unconscious and woke up in a couple of minutes sitting in his seat and still strapped to the seat, sailing through the air. He just unbuckled his safety belt and stepped out of the seat into space and then pulled his ripcord. Another guy I knew fell into a building and went through the roof and landed in a pen full of pigs. Another officer who was a navigator jumped out of his plane and was hit on the head by the horizontal stabilizer and was out for three weeks. He did not remember a thing until he woke up in prison camp. Others landed and attempted to escape. I recall the bombardier on our crew hid out for several days in some farmland but was soon captured along a railway track by the train crew. Another guy evaded the Germans for about two weeks by living in haystacks and stealing chickens at night. He boiled these up with a little fire in the daytime, but grew so weak from lack of salt he had to give himself up.

During the long dark nights, the one activity that was always present and always kept reminding a person we were in a prison was the constant play of the silent searchlights. The guards, as they watched from the tall wooden towers, would stand behind the searchlight and slowly play the lights over the compound. The searching spotlights would play along the wall, over the windows and then under the barracks that had been built on stilts.

Whenever they detected a sound they would rapidly move the searchlight over to the place of the probable activity. The Kriegies became accustomed to these lights and it became a part of the life within the prison camp. During the winter when it was cold outside and snow was on the ground, they seemed to have a strange psychological effect on the men. It made all the men more lonesome for home and within their minds it raised the question of how and when this war would end.

Discipline and organization in the room

I do feel that within the ordinary POW barracks room with 24 men, discipline and organization reached a well-developed level of use and purpose. The rooms were relatively small, about 20 x 26 feet.

On at least a dozen occasions I was in a position to take 24 new Kriegies and assign them to a barracks room, which had just been completed. I would then brief the men for a few minutes on the basic responsibilities they had in the room, when the coal would be issued, the time of the next roll call, when rations would be distributed by the ration officer, and gave them a general outline as to how they could organize their room. It was interesting that within minutes an organizational structure complete with authority, discipline, and assignment of duties would take place. The Kriegies would feel each other out as to where to sleep, where to put things, and shortly a strong air of cooperation solved their mutual problems. Generally speaking, the organization in the room was not based on authority but on cooperation. The minute one Kriegie attempted to take advantage of another Kriegie, such as in a sleeping arrangement, the other 23 men politely and firmly advised the man there were 24 equal men in the room. Nothing more would be said. Military rank, wealth, status, size, brains, ability, and a big mouth were no longer determining factors in his life.

Within an hour after moving into the new room, an air of peace, quiet, and understanding fell over the room. Within a day it became home. I think much of the understanding and cooperation and good will and concern expressed for another took place the first day or two after dark when Kriegies went to bed. They then began exploring themselves and soon a level of tolerance and understanding was established which made the room full of men a cohesive unit; "all for one, one for all."

To the best of my knowledge, this cooperation continued as long as the men remained assigned together in the room. I can never recall a man asking permission to move to another room or stating he did not like his room. He became part of 23 other men and they became part of him.

I cannot recall any permanent personal conflict in the air within the room, which made for bitterness. I can never recall any fights between Kriegies; though there would be arguments. The level of emotions was, in some way, always controlled. Perhaps the other 22 men in the room controlled the mood. In a room filled with men you always had a jury sitting and listening and with many men it is impossible to put some thing over on another man.

The question comes up about selfishness. In each man's mind the word means something different. I do feel that the opposite word, "unselfishness", in its broadest sense, was a strong characteristic of all Kriegies. Despite the fact that all men had various ranks, there was still an unparalleled equality. The goal for every man was the same and all men looked at the next man and understood his inner thoughts.

One of the reasons for the cooperation in the barracks room was many of the items that cause trouble between men had been removed from the environment; women, sex, money, personal possessions, family, status, liquor, physical and mental ability, and last, but not least, a man's ego was controlled not by himself but by 23 other prisoners.

Here in the prisoner barracks, a man could look at himself. If you were the son of the president of General Motors, the son of the Secretary of War, the son of a father on welfare, or the son of an unknown it made no difference; we were all equal. A situation like this would be impossible to imagine in contemporary society in the United States. The men in the room thought as equals and they treated each other as equals.

It may be noticed so many times I keep coming back to the life and society within the Kriegie room. If you placed 24 men from all walks of life in a room in the States, I know you would have turmoil, jealousy and competition. In normal life the environment play a great part in one's actions, while in Kriegie camp one's heredity comes to the forefront in his behavior.

The Kriegies themselves had a number of unwritten rules and regulations that applied to their own conduct. These were not set forth by the Germans or by the Senior American officers in camp. They were established on the basis of the so-called Golden Rule and were based on the principal of the protection of the weakest against the strongest. An example would be the right of property. Whatever possession you may have, such as a candy bar, a pencil, a can of dried milk, you could lay it on your bed in full view of all the men and feel free to leave your room all day and still be a hundred percent certain it would be on your bed when you returned. I can never recall an instance of any meaningful item being stolen from another man. It just never crossed our minds to steal from another person. There were two good reasons for this. If you should steal something from your peers they would deal out punishment and there was no maximum punishment. I believe if a Kriegie had been caught stealing a Red Cross parcel the other Kriegies would have waited until dark and they would have twisted his head around until his body stilled and they would have dumped the body out the barracks window. There would be no recourse. The killing of that Kriegie in the camp would not be an act of cruelty. Instead it would be an act of protection for all the other men. There could not be nor would there be an exception, for example, on stealing food which was the "staff of life."

Another fact which made conduct between the Kriegies proper was if you poked a cruel form of fun at another Kriegie, the other POWs in the room would firmly advise you not to pursue the matter further. This would end the matter because you had no escape from your prosecutors. It was also extremely important you do nothing to embarrass or hurt any other Kriegie either directly or indirectly. That is why the senior Allied officers in your compound must first approve any plans for escape, barter, trade, etc. with the German guards. A man's action could, in many cases result, in punishment for all the POWs. For example, one Kriegie could, by devious ways, throw off the roll call count for the Germans, in which case all the men would have to stand at attention for another 30 minutes outside in the cold while the Germans recounted the entire camp. This would be a fine act to harass the enemy, but the welfare of 9,000 men, poorly dressed, standing in the snow for a long period of time, would have to be weighed against the value of the act.

It may be recalled that earlier I mentioned that sex is not important. I shall explain this.

To explain this is difficult because all men are so intertwined with women in thought, word, and deed. When the chips are down in life, reproduction takes a second place. Life itself is most important in an individual's mind. Reproduction or the relationship with women is a sophisticated relationship which appears only after a person has satisfied his own needs for life. When his need is satisfied, he exerts himself to reproduce in kind. I think the above facts have been well documented in history.

In all self-contained societies, food plays the predominant factor in population control.

Sex and reproduction are only by-products of life. Man's and woman's first duty is to live and survive and attend to the simple duties of relationships between persons.

Men and women, in themselves, are selfish and greedy. To say they like each other and cooperate is questionable. Every person looks out for himself. If there is anything left we go out for the raising of families.

A person may think with hundreds of men, women and dirty jokes would play a major part of their lives. This was not true. Sex is a very sophisticated part of a man's life. Some may say it is natural or instinctive. This may be true, but nature and instinct take a back set to survival.

Time after time I have noticed and observed the first desire—the first and foremost interest—of man is food and water. Then comes shelter, then clothes to keep you warm, then friendship to help you emotionally. Perhaps women would think differently. This I do not know.

It would be very interesting, from a psychological point of view, to put 10,000 women in a confined compound, observe their actions, and listen to their desires and wants. It could well be women would have a strong desire for men. Then again, they may have little interest.

Life as a Prisoner Of War

The ritual of prison life was slowly evolving. Gradually the little things that had once seemed strange and queer were becoming a part of everyday living.

One of the keys to living was to be able to fill up the hours you were awake with some type of action or thinking that would keep you sound in mind and spirit. Since we were officers, we were not allowed to work. I don't know how important this factor was in the scheme of the German Prisoner of War program, but when you a new work program was begun, the Germans would immediately run into complications, such as needing many more guards, transportation, clothing for variations in weather, supply and logistic problems.

The few heavy duty chores required around camp were handled by Russian Prisoners of War. The Germans did not consider rank in the Russian Army and as far as the Germans were concerned, the Russian POWs were all Buck Privates.

Across the road from our camp, the Germans maintained about 300 Russian officers who were used to do the menial tasks around the camp including digging potatoes on the prison farm. I recall once in our room the little tin stove pipe going up through the roof broke and needed repair. The Germans sent a Russian Colonel who had been flying Sturmovick fighter planes and had been shot down. He repaired the pipe as the German guard watched over him.

Many times in instances such as this, when the Russian, the German, and a few American Kriegies were together for a few minutes, there was an air of cordiality. For example, we would ask the German Private how he felt to be guarding a Russian Colonel, or we would ask the Russian what he was going to do after the war. How many pounds of weight had he gained on the German menu? One big question was when the war would end. We had to watch ourselves in situations like this because it certainly was not beyond reason that if we went too far the German guard could report us. In a case like, this the guard would not carry a rifle or pistol because with several Kriegies around him it would be very easy for us to secure the weapon. A good axiom of prison life is for the guard never to carry keys, weapons, or any instrument that could be taken away and used against themselves.

As soon as we got a German guard alone, such as in the case of the Russian POW Colonel repairing the stove pipe, we always applied a little subtle pressure. For example, in this case, we would ask the German if he wanted a cigarette. Obviously, he would say no. Trading with a prisoner was a certain way for the guard to be shot in the morning. What we would do is to take an open cigarette pack out and lay it on the table next to the Guard, then we would all leave the room and close the door. He did not know if we had counted the cigarettes. The Guard did not know if we would report him, we literally put him in a position that was nearly irresistible. Before the Guard and the Russian left, we would slip the Russian a pack of cigarettes. Cigarettes were worth their weight in gold in a prisoner of war camp. It was not necessary that you smoke because they had such a high value for trade purposes.

Around the first of the year in 1945, South Four Compound opened up. In picking the staff for the new compound, which was a combination of military rank and politics within the camp, Captain Blackburn was assigned as one of the Block Commanders, and he selected me as the second in command, or A administrative Officer. My principal duty was to keep an official account of who lived in the barracks by rank, serial number, and name. In addition, during roll call, I aided the German officer in searching the building and assisted in making the German roll call jibe with the German and American records.

In this case I had a big advantage during the winter because I would not have to stand outside for roll call. Consequently, I had some small talk with the German guard each day, although I could not speak German and he could not speak English. Most of the time the German guard was old and was little more than a figurehead. I was in a position to take his rifle and shoot him. He was aware of this and we attempted to cooperate within a reasonable mask of military duties between enemy and prisoners. As the war neared its end, the last few days the guard would cry as he looked through the barracks and made his count. He was 100% at my mercy and, despite the fact he did not speak my language, he visibly pleaded for my mercy, forgiveness, and above all, his life, through his eyes. Soon the war would end and the Russians would probably shoot him.

The most comical thing in the camp was the hauling out of the latrine sewage. The Germans used a horse drawn sewage tank which had a long rubber hose attached to the back of the tank. This large hose was dropped into the latrine sewage and then the inside of the tank was sprayed with gasoline. A spark was set off in the tank and there would be an explosion. A trap door on top of the tank flipped up and then closed rapidly, forming a vacuum in the tank, and this vacuum sucked up the sewage from the latrine hole in the ground.

Something always was going wrong with this contraption. Perhaps the trap door would fail to open or close, the two old horses would buck and run away or back up, a harness would break, once a wheel fell off, one time the tank slid back into the hole in the ground. Something always happened. There would always be a constant stream of German swearing from the poor guards who were attempting to operate the outfit. This whole show was carried on much to the delight of hundreds of Kriegies. Sometimes things went so badly for the poor German guard that out of mercy we would help him when he was at his wit's end. Prison life can sometimes be funny.

About once every two weeks the German guards would conduct what was called a picture parade and search the barracks room by room. This search consisted of two guards entering a room with a deck of cards, each card contained a man's picture, his name, and his German P.O.W. serial number. The guard would read off your name and then you would reply by giving your serial number. This serial number was the number assigned to you when you entered the German Prisoner of War organization. My number was 6135. This apparently was a double check on the daily roll calls and would be conducted at random.

During this so-called picture parade, the Germans would conduct a cursory search of the room. This was conducted in a rapid and business like manner. They would look into the corners and under beds, under the thin mattresses, into the food and coal boxes, into library books, and into the stove. This would go rapidly because they may have a hundred rooms to go through during the evening. The primary instrument used in all searches was a long thin steel rod; this was about an eighth of an inch in diameter and three feet long. With it, they probed the mattress, the cracks in the wall, ashes in the stove, and the many places they could not reach with their hands.

During some of the picture parades at night, one would run into a mean guard who would go out of his way to destroy some little personal objects a Kriegie may have spent many hours making. Some of these objects could include a little model plane out of wood, a little diary relating some of the experiences or thoughts of the prisoner, pictures a person would have drawn, perhaps a small object of art cut out of a bar of soap and so on. These small acts of destruction were bitterly resented by the prisoners. In my own case, they never did destroy any little objects I had made because they had been hidden well. In addition, the German guards were aware I was second in command of 250 officers.

While in camp I attempted to make a few notes each day. I had one advantage in that the Prisoner who was in charge of the meager pencil and paper supply slept next to me in the barracks. This officer was a Lt. Ray from Tennessee, a lawyer by profession. He and I were good friends. I didn't take advantage of our friendship, but I did always have a little paper to write on. The pencil was not too important because you could always make ink and make yourself a pen with which to write. The paper, incidentally, was issued by the Red Cross, rather than by the Germans.

Despite the fact we were in a prison camp, we did have one big inspection that would remind anyone of an annual inspection in an Army Camp. This was the time the International Red Cross representatives from Sweden visited the camp in March, 1945. The German Officers in charge of the Camp were most desirous of making a good impression and as a result the Germans issued us extra food for our cooperation in making the camp presentable. It was the one time we washed the floors, washed our clothes, and had every room in reasonable shape. The inspecting party consisted of several Swedish Generals and high ranking civilians from Sweden, and a few other neutral countries were also represented. The inspection turned out fine and, of course, nothing better or nothing worse came as a result of the inspection. Camp returned to normal the next day.

In making a few notes each day relative to some activity or thoughts while in camp, I noticed there was a direct relationship concerning the amount I wrote and the amount of food we had available. If we had only a small bowl of soup, I would, perhaps write nothing or just a sentence at the most. If we had a bowl of barley soup, my writing would extend to a couple of sentences. If we had a reasonable meal, it would extend to half a page. When it was very cold and, because of cramped quarters, the act of writing sometimes took more physical effort and space than was available. Because of the limited paper supply, almost all the notes I made were written on the back of the cigarette package paper. This makes fairly good writing paper and was small enough so it could be hidden and was easily put away.

One of the favorite pastimes in the camp was playing cards and, in most instances this would be bridge, whist, and gin rummy, or the many variations of the rummy games. One advantage to rummy was the game could be stopped or started at any time and the number of players could vary as the day and night wore on. I vividly recall playing a gin rummy game with Lt. Glass from Dallas, Texas. We set our goal that the winner had to have 10,000 points. This game took about four weeks of playing, off and on, and he eventually won by a narrow margin.

There were a few regular decks of cards in camp, but most had been made out of the cardboard boxes in which we received our Red Cross parcels. The quality of the cards made little difference because after you play with some poor cards, you get accustomed to it then and you always look for the high numbers even if the quality of the card is poor.

Card tricks were also a big item, and one of the unwritten rules in any kind of card trick or any trick for that matter, was you only played the trick once and then it was up to your buddies to figure it out. Obviously, if you show the same trick a few times, anyone can catch on, but if you only show the new trick once you have a real problem on your hands.

One of the intriguing things about camp life was the news, how it came to camp, how it was distributed. In our camp the Germans maintained a bulletin board on which they scrawled in chalk a brief sketch of the German official news. This only pointed up a review of the German successes for the past 24 hours.

The Americans in Camp published a secret daily newspaper called the "POW WOW". The paper was put together in some unknown part of the camp. It was type written, single spaced, covering one full sheet of yellow onion skin paper. The additional copies were carbon copies. This paper was secretly picked up by the compound Intelligence Officer late in the afternoon, usually at the time rations were distributed. In the evening, after the lights were out, the paper was read by candle light and passed from one room to another. The paper was of exceptional quality in that it had no purpose except to give the news as it was received. In addition, it gave only the official news of each country as of midnight each night. It had no editorial comment, no rewriting, no guesses, and no impressions. It was and is the only newspaper I know of that was ever published which gave only official news. It gave the official broadcast of news in full of the United States, England, Germany and Russia. If the news was important, good, bad, propaganda, or whatever, this was left up to the intelligence of the reader.

We noted, with a touch of humor or irony, that we knew a great deal more about what was happening in the world than did Americans recently shot down or our German guards. I know of no group of people in a war who had full access to all sides of the fighting and were able to sit back and make a reasonable evaluation of the situation. For example, the large daily newspaper in the United States in World War II had very little information and presented little news compared to what our newspaper published. The Kriegies in Stalag Luft I had the finest newspaper published during World War II. If you only listened and read only the news of one country, which is what most people did, they lived the war in blissful ignorance.

To this date I am sure the source of the newspaper was never found and destroyed by the Germans because it was too valuable to them. The Kriegies had built their own short wave receiving sets and I am sure the Germans knew this, but they were just as hungry for unadulterated news as anyone. In the camp, the Germans put on a big show about once a month of looking for the source of this newspaper and the hidden radio or radios. I feel in my own mind the paper was allowed to be published with the understanding that the German Camp Commander was given the first copy.

In addition to the Camp Newspaper the Senior Allied officers apparently had access to secret information from outside Germany through agents who operated in the area. I, as an ordinary prisoner, was never privy to any of these going on. However, in the room where I lived we did have the Block Intelligence Officer who was in on reasonably high intelligence meetings and passed on information. For example, Hitler, at one time, had ordered us all killed in retaliation for an Allied air raid on Dresden, Germany. The Germans were busy converting the shower room pipes for the installation of gas. Our camp was going to be one of the strong points of resistance in front of the Russian Armies. The Russians would have to blast us out of the way to get to the Germans. This operation never became a reality. The war ended too soon.

Christmas, to the Germans, is a very important celebration, and part of this good will filtered down to the Kriegies. In addition, almost everyone saved some food so everyone could have a good meal on Christmas Eve. On this occasion, the only one while I was a prisoner, we were allowed to assemble in a relatively large group. The American officers held the Christmas party for our compound in the German kitchen-dining room. I suppose there were about 2,500 in attendance. The program consisted mainly of singing Christmas songs.

One reason the evening was so memorable was the thought that back in the room we had saved up extra food to eat Christmas Eve. It was miserable to be hungry, but to know back in the room we would eat a good meal was the most wonderful thought in the world. The highlight of the program was the singing by four officers of a number of Christmas carols. These four Kriegies had made home brew from raisins and prunes and were feeling high when they began singing. After a couple of numbers, they took another round of drinks. After a dozen carols they were on top of the world and they sang Christmas carols as they have never been sung before. As they became more "under the influence" the Kriegies egged them on for more song and they gave it their all, in voice, melody, and soul. May God forgive them.

In the evening we went back to the barracks and in high spirits, we prepared our meal. After the meal the dishes were washed and we all went to bed with full stomachs and reveled in our physical and mental happiness.

One of the sad incidents was during the early evening following the full meal in our room, two Kriegies got sick and had to vomit up the entire meal. I just can't describe how sorry we felt for them or how sorry these guys felt for themselves. After the war ended, several men ate themselves to death because the stomach could not digest food. They ended up in convulsions and died.

Church services, on a formal basis, were conducted by an English Padre (Chaplain) of the Church of England. He had been captured when the British Army was forced to evacuate at Dunkirk. These services were conducted each Sunday, outside during warm weather, and in the German dining hall in the winter. There were a large number of denominations in the camp, and many of these smaller denominations held short informal meetings or services in individual rooms in each block. The Catholics, being a larger group, usually would also meet in the German dining hall. The Kriegies were forbidden to hold large gatherings, demonstrate, sing in groups, dance or sing their National Anthem.

We had one large meeting in the Camp shortly after I arrived, when an Air Force Colonel by the name of Spicer called all the Americans together in one compound and talked about various subjects, one being the Germans were not treating us fairly or humanly. As a result, he was automatically thrown in solitary confinement for two weeks. I recall as soon as he finished his speech two German officers escorted him directly out of our Compound to solitary.

An interesting religious experience for all the men in the prison camp occurred near the end of the war. In our camp of about 10,000 men, there were several hundred Jews from the British and American Air Forces. These men had received no special attention and therefore were blended in the camp with the other men. In our compound of 2,500 men, I would say there were about 30 Jews. One day there appeared on the bulletin board a short memorandum which read that all the prisoners who were Jewish should sign their name on a blank sheet of paper. It went on to say these men were no longer considered Americans or British prisoners and would be removed from the camp. It further added the Germans did not have a listing of Jewish men, consequently the only men that would be removed from the camp would be those who signed their name on the list.

It was a foregone conclusion these men would be killed or sent to a concentration camp, which would be the same thing. The memorandum on the board concluded their names must be on the list within 72 hours.

In discussing this notice and the results with other officers it was questionable how many would sign the list. To our surprise, I would judge about 25 Jews signed the list out of the 30 in our compound. A person would have to have a very strong religious and cultural belief to sign what amounted to a certain death certificate.

Within the minds of the other Kriegies most of which were of various sects of the Christian belief it became a question if they would have signed this list; if, rather than Jews, they had asked for Christians to sign the list. It would be very unlikely any member of the Christian faith would have such a strong belief that he would have made public his faith in Christianity if it meant he would die as a result of his public confession.

It was an interesting side light to prison life to learn there are men in this world willing to die for their beliefs and culture. I feel sure this would not be true of Christians, regardless of the faith they may confess or profess. There are obviously thousands of Christians who have and will die for their belief in Christ. I do feel the circumstances in the above case were unusual.

It was interesting to note the physical and mental health in the camp was very high. I cannot recall any Kriegie requiring the services of a doctor or dentist while in camp. I cannot recall a dentist being in camp, but I suppose they did have one. The camp doctor was a Negro native of South Africa who had been captured in North Africa by General Rommel's Afrika Korps. He maintained a dispensary and hospital with three or four beds and a few drugs. I recall the rumor going around from time to time that the doctor was making surveys to determine if any Kriegies wanted their appendix out so he could maintain his skill and practice in surgery. Within each compound, with from 2,000 to 3,000 men, one American first aid man was issued some bandages and Aspirin to take care of the day to day medical needs. The Germans, at least in the camp, were great believers in Aspirin. If a person had any thing wrong, cut, sprain, cramps, or what not, the standard German treatment was Aspirin period! If a man was bleeding they would give aspirin plus a small bandage and that was it.

The hospital did have one thing and that was food. The Germans and Americans did maintain an above average food supply, and this would usually take care of most sick men admitted to the hospital. A few men did have nervous breakdowns or suffered from some form of mental illness. One officer in our block refused to get out of bed for months at a time. Another, I recall, was always talking about some big deal he wanted us in on. Some of the Kriegies had been hit pretty hard on the head by the horizontal stabilizer on the plane when leaving the plane so there was a reason for the mental upset. If they got out of hand, the Germans would take them away and that was the last we ever heard of them. I never heard Kriegies complain about health. All they wanted was food; they wanted food more than freedom, and it seemed as if the only reason many wanted freedom was to be able to eat.

I did have an infection in my lower jaw bone, but the infection was open and a small amount of pus would come out. The pain was not severe and I had it corrected when I arrived back in the States. I did lose some teeth as a result of this bone infection.

Liquor in the Prisoner of War camp was limited, to say the least. This is one item I can never recall being received from the Germans through blackmail or barter. The Germans did have some beer, but due to the poor quality, it was never bought or sold in the infamous guard and prisoner exchange schemes. I can recall as stated previously, we were issued beer only once and it was of poor quality, that is, if you consider alcoholic content a part of quality.

The Kriegies were ingenious in making their own alcoholic brew. The Red Cross parcels they usually had a small package of prunes. Some of the Kriegies would take and cut them up into small pieces, add some sugar and set them under a bed and let them ferment. In about two or three weeks the resulting juice would contain some alcohol to one degree or another. Occasionally, other chemical compounds developed such as formaldehyde. However the Kriegies would drink the resulting brew with varied results. Sometimes this brew caused a wonderful drunkenness, sometimes a temporary blindness, sometimes a paralysis, but always something. Usually the brew was made and reserved for holidays. The most famous or infamous occasion was the Christmas party when the four drunken Kriegies sang the Christmas carols.

After the Russians liberated us, the Russians and Kriegies went on forays to secure liquor or what not from the local population. A few adventurous Kriegies then stole or confiscated liquor from the German citizens and some really went to town. Usually they ended up laying in a street or field. They just drank themselves into an unconscious stupor.

The German Army, as far as I could see, was well disciplined and well trained. The first thing that struck me when I came in contact with them was the quality of their uniform. The material was of high quality and wrinkle proof.

Stalag Luft I was a German Air Force Camp, controlled and administered by the German Air Force (Luftwaffe). I often thought after the war, regardless of the reparation, it would be nice if the United States Air Force would take the Basic German Air Force uniform and make it the official U.S. Air Force uniform. It was light green in color, and made of pure wool. It was modest, business-like, military-like, and always presented an air of dignity. The German boots were of superior quality, and tended to lend an air of authority and style to the wearer. The German officers' leather coats were tops. They were black, soft, smooth leather and I have never seen a coat in the United States to compare in quality nor any garment that gave the wearer the style and class of a real leather black coat.

The scheme the Germans used in denoting rank and ribbons of battle and courage were also very clear and neat. The United States formulated its own uniform, ribbons, and insignia, as a result of the break away from the European military system, so of course there could be no return to the system. The picture that most often returns to my mind is the German officer walking in the rain with his leather coat, the water shed from his hat, coat, and boots as if the rain were not intended for him. To one who has seen this, it is a sight of authority that is hard to forget.

One important sideline to prison life was the mail you theoretically could send and receive. In accordance with the Geneva Convention, we were allowed to send three post cards each month and four letters. A person never knows until after a war that just because you wrote letters does not mean they will be delivered. In my childish thoughts I just assumed they would be delivered. Edwina received a couple of cards and a couple of letters. Conversely, Edwina was extended the same mailing privileges that I was. During my stay in prison camp I received one letter and two parcels of cigarettes. The letter I did receive was a most treasured possession. I read it hundreds of times and all the officers in the room read it over and read into it the meanings they would want from their own wives and girl friends. There were four cartons of Lucky Strikes in each tobacco package. I received one with which I bought, or in everyday language, I traded, a pair of British Army shoes. My shoes were worn out and no good. It was a status symbol to have a pair of British shoes and these I had always treasured so I bought a pair.

I recall they had hob nails over the heels and soles and made a person feel important. The British Army shoes were not new but they were in good shape. I wore them every day until I arrived home in Fairdale.

The dress in prison camp was most interesting. It was the only way one could express himself and maintain a self respecting ego complex. First the hair dress. It was a United States Air Force unwritten rule that the hair must be neat and presentable and free of lice. You could cut or comb your hair in any way you desired. Combs were scarce but each room would have at least one comb.

In the cutting of the hair the Kriegies showed a talent for originality and ability far and beyond anything that normal men could create. Obviously, there have been many hair styles through history, but here was a time and place when the individual could create fashions that would remain as different in hair styling. Each man had a different cut. There was only one pair of scissors to each two hundred or three hundred men and the scissors passed from room to room. There were no clippers, thinners, razors, etc. In describing the hair cuts it is well to remind you long hair was not possible because of the hair and body lice. Consequently, most hair styles were relatively short. Many a man attempted to have created on his head an image or symbol which he wanted to present to the other Kriegies.

Many cut their hair into comical designs such as a cross, ribbons, a bowl, or just a tuft of hair coming out on top. Some cut the hair into circles, some cut it all off on top and let it grow around the ears. There were hundreds of variations and each would be an interesting design. In the contemporary styles of society there are no variations because all people conform to what they think is a style. When one sees a person with long hair, about the only connotation that can be drawn is he did not cut his hair. About the most radical hair styles in contemporary society consist of limiting the growth in some manner on the head or face. Modern society does not provide a very fertile ground for the man with initiative or talent to be different. All that can be said, is he wants to look like everybody else.

The clothing worn by the Kriegie also presented a contrast with modern society. The Kriegies, as officers, always attempted to wear their clothing in a neat and appealing manner. The officer who did not wash his pants or shirt was politely told to clean up and he did. Pants were pressed by sleeping on them and they looked good. The most distinctive feature of the Kriegie dress was that all Kriegies always wore the pants inside the stocking above the shoe. This was the most comfortable and presented the neatest appearance in a group. The stocking was always rolled down, then the pants folded tight around the leg and the stocking rolled up over the pants leg. Then the excess of pants was bloused over the stocking. This is very comfortable and neat.

I have used the word Kriegie to describe a Prisoner of War. All prisoners always refer to themselves as Kriegies and anything that had a connection with prisoner of war was prefaced by the word Kriegie. Consequently, bread was referred to as Kriegie bread, the stove was referred to as a Kriegie stove, stories told about the war were known as Kriegie stories.

When I arrived at our camp the average age of the guards was about 45 years and as the war progressed the men were shipped out and replaced by older men. The average age towards the end of the war was between 65 to 70 years. The guards were sent to the Russian front because that was where the pressure was, that was where the terrible fighting was taking place. The guards hated the Russians and going to the Russian front was the equivalent of a death sentence. This fact was used by the Commanders at camp to maintain a very tight and strict discipline among the guards.

After a guard had been in camp for a month or so, the prisoners would have him well sized up, and most of the guards were ordinary, average men. They treated us like men and we treated them like men. In a prison camp, a strange rapport develops between the guards and the prisoners.

The Camp was located only about 100 yards from the Baltic Ocean, therefore the climate was moist but not severe. The fall was nice, but from November through February there was snow on the ground and January and February the temperature hovered near zero all the time. March and April were cool and May was nice. One of the problems was, because we were so near the ocean we were subject to low lying coastal clouds and fog much of the time. This kept the humidity high and in the winter it was very uncomfortable because we did not have any heat in the buildings. A fact that added to the oppressive nature of the weather was the sun did not shine much in the winter and thus added dark gloom over the camp.

An interesting intelligence problem was solved when new Kriegies would arrive in camp. The American or Allied commanders in camp had strict instructions that no one would talk or associate with a new Kriegie unless he could be positively identified by an American Air Force officer. This was an American Air Force directive.

The Germans used a lot of tricks to move men into the camp who would pass as American or British POWs and then go around the camp and gather military intelligence. After these men had secured some information, they would be rapidly removed by the Germans. Consequently, to solve the problem, it was a standing rule in the camp that all prisoners of war must be positively identified by another U.S. Army Air Force officer and bona fide Kriegie. This process started as soon as the new Kriegies were moved into camp and usually the new Kriegies were not aware of the process. As the new men, say a hundred or so, moved into camp, we would line up along the barbed wire and note the ones we knew and as soon as they had been assigned to a room we would report the man's name to the Compound Intelligence Officer who would then clear the man. We were always able to clear all the men and the process would only take about two hours. When you get 10,000 Air Force men together, the chances would be certain you would know some of the new officers, so this identification was a simple routine process. A fake or stooge would stand out in a few minutes and the Germans would yank him out of camp for his own protection shortly. Towards the end of the war they cut out this child's play.

The average Kriegie wore one stocking cap, one old soldier's (US) or RAF overcoat, lead regulation or POW wings, shirt and trousers and long underwear, socks were worn over pants, and rank insignia was made from tin cans.

The manufacture of lead wings and insignia provided an interesting, time consuming and skilled pastime. The lead was recovered from the food cans we received. A small forge, complete with bellows to provide high heat, would be built utilizing the stove as the foundation and frame. The lead from many cans would then be melted in the forge. After the fire cooled all the lead particles would be recovered and melted again in an iron cup and the impurities skimmed off. Then a small mold made of wet fine sand would be imprinted with a set of wings, and the hot molten lead poured into the form. Then thin wires or other items would be inserted into the back of the hot metal to form some type of clasp. These wings sold for about two chocolate bars of candy. However, the cost would go down in direct ratio to the amount of lead or labor one would put into the project. This became an art and some of the officers who became skilled at the procedure profited and would make a couple of sets in one week. The securing of the lead from the cans was a major problem. There is not very much lead in a little tin can, just a drop

Regarding the German police dogs that were used at night by the guards in patrolling the compounds, a rather bizarre incident happened one winter night. The dogs were only used at night when all the men were locked up in the blocks or barracks. The night guards patrolled without guns or weapons, with only the dog on the end of a ten foot, black leather leash.

This particular night the men in one of the rooms had opened the window shouting some sarcastic remark at the guard each time he made his rounds by a certain block. The guard thought he would get even with them, so next time he passed by the window and a Kriegie shouted something, the guard let the angry dog go, ordering him to jump up and in through the open window. The guard waited patiently outside the window, which has been closed as soon as the dog jumped in. Everything was quiet. The guard waited for about forty five minutes and then the windows opened and two Kriegies approached the window and gently threw the full skeleton, with all the bones attached, showing the dog-shaped skeleton, out through the window and it landed at the feet of the guard with the long black leather strap still attached around the neck bones. The entire incident was hushed up by the Germans and instructions were issued to the guards to preclude further incidents such as this happening again. By the way, the Kriegies made stew out of the dog so the incident served a two fold purpose.

The English Chaplain we had in camp had the longest list of verses in the English language to the famous drinking song "I Used to Work in Chicago". On occasions in the camp, when a group of men gathered for some type of recreation such as a Christmas party, he would really let go and lead the group in singing the endless verses he had in his repertoire. Every time I think of the Chaplain, I think of the time he was visiting in our room and I had just finished distilling and manufacturing a small quantity of ink in a tin cup.

Ink was hard to make. I manufactured it out of purple cabbage; by only using the blue cabbage leaves and then slowly boiling and distilling the fluid you would eventually end up with a dark purple substance with an ink like quality that could be used in home made pens for writing. The quickest and best way to make ink was to trade with the German guards for an indelible pencil. Then grind up the lead and mix it with water. This really worked well and was much faster to make, than the homemade purple cabbage process.

I would judge the mental health of the prisoners was excellent. There were several reasons for this. One factor was, as a prisoner, one is sheltered from many of the factors in normal life back in the states that would cause trouble and anxiety. For example, there was no job to worry about, nor promotions or advancements, nor wives or girl friends, no money, nothing to buy, no keeping up with the Jones's, no car troubles; you couldn't flunk out of the institution nor was there any way you could really fail in your own eyes or in the eyes of your peers and friends. This reduced living to an elementary level and made life simple. It also had its disadvantages as far as mental health is concerned because when a man started to worry about something, there was so little to stop his chain of thinking that he soon became obsessed with the thought. He did not have other mental problems to carry his thinking into other areas. On two or three occasions, men came to me with what I thought were very small problems but the poor guys had become overwhelmed with their thinking and I noticed if they had a chance to talk to someone it all cleared up in a very few days and they could rationalize themselves.

I was surprised at the rapid adjustment men can make under severe conditions. Not only does the body adjust but the mind adjusts quickly to a new set of circumstances. In addition, I do feel a man gains strength from other men. Consequently, one man tends to support another. In the prison camp I detected some competition but very little as compared to a normal society. There was strong evidence of cooperation among the men at all times during camp stay.

One thing that irritated me was the way Lt. Ainsworth would wash his clothes. To the other guys, they just did not give a damn how he washed his clothes, but when Lt. Ainsworth washed, he irritated me. Lt. Ainsworth lived in our room and was the Block Intelligence Officer or, in Air Force parlance, the S-1 Officer. I was always trying to help him and he paid no attention to my suggestions. When he washed he would put his olive drab pants, long underwear, socks, brown shirt, and everything he owned into a pail which had been filled with water, a little Ivory soap, and some homemade lye. This he would put between his legs and with a Kriegie made clothes stomper, he would pump up and down for hours. All his clothes, consequently, turned the same color—a sort of dirty brown. He was always wondering why his white clothes did not come out white and I told him he could not mix colored clothes and he told me I knew nothing about washing, and this is the way his mother had washed clothes back in Texas for 25 years. I told him he was all wrong and she never mixed the clothes when washing. He thought I was stupid and was casting a reflection on his mother. He never did figure out why his underwear was brown. That reminds me, he still owes me fifteen dollars from a deal we made.

In regards to injuries many of the men suffered during the process of being shot down, the most prominent were the men that had been crippled. Following the injury, the Germans, in many cases, would take a man to a hospital and provide reasonable care in setting broken bones and medicating fresh wounds. In many cases, joints, such as the knee and elbow that were injured were treated by a standard procedure which was to immobilize the joint to ease the pain and knowing the man did not have to work in prison camp he would be sent there with his stiff joint. I suppose most of these injuries or deformities were corrected in state side hospital following the war.

In each compound they had a small, I repeat, small, library with perhaps 1000 books. These had been sent by the Red Cross in the States and provided a diversion to the long days and evenings. Some of the books which I read while in camp were: "Kamet Conquered", "Christ's Life and Teachings", "Social Aspects of Religion", "Poems by James Whitcomb Riley", "Old Mother Earth", "2222 Questions and Answers", "Public Speaking Speeches", "On Being a Real Person", "A Naturalist in Nicaragua", "Twelve Tests of Character", "Works of Ralph Waldo Emerson", "The Home of the Blizzard", "Select Magazine 1923", "Races of Africa", and "The Soul in Being". These are listed as an example of the type of reading material in the camp and as can be seen, it was reasonably adequate. The big problem was getting into the Library, which was about 12 feet by 12 feet and always jammed. It just wasn't worth the fight to get a book when it took all afternoon. There were a few German propaganda books in the Library, perhaps by accident rather than design. The books could only be kept a couple of days so it was hard to read someone else's book because he would have to return it in 48 hours.

There were no so called recreation facilities. Anyone familiar with a Prisoner of War camp will know prisoners will not exert any unnecessary energy in useless recreational activities. A person must conserve all his strength and a game like volleyball would be the height of folly. A prisoner did need some exercise to keep from getting stiff but this exercise consisted of walking around the compound. The prisoners liked to walk at a slow, leisurely pace. With this many men in the small area there was not a blade of grass on the ground. If there had been any grass the Kriegies would have pulled it and eaten it or made some type of liquor out of it. The Kriegie minds were fertile sources of information and they would stop at nothing to make whatever was needed or sometimes they would make something just because it presented a challenge to their minds.

Despite long hours in camp, I cannot recall any other prisoner writing down any facts or notes in a notebook. I am sure there were some, but I never did hear of them, nor did I hear a rumor of such activity. I should stress it is difficult to make notes in a prison camp unless you discipline yourself. One problem was every day seemed exactly like the next day or the day before and it seemed as if there was nothing to put down on paper. Another factor is when a person is hungry it just seems too useless to write, for all a person can think about is food. Also, the little things are happening around you in the room such as card playing, visiting, arguing, talking about food, wondering if the Germans had the water turned on in the washroom, how a guy evaded the Germans for ten days before he was captured, when or how the war would end, and what they were going to eat on the first day they arrived back in the states. These items seem meaningless and stupid to put on paper. An analogy could be drawn by attempting to recall who you know in contemporary society who sits down once a day or once a week and writes down how the events of the world have looked in his eyes during the past day or week. It just is not logical.

In prisoner of war life there is a well balanced scale of behavior on the part of all parties concerned. The guards were always in command, but soon the Kriegies determined just exactly what behavior was expected and what type of behavior would be tolerated. It is interesting that the guard's behavior was always visible and all prisoners knew what the guards were doing and thinking, but the guards did not know what the prisoners were up to because so much of the Kriegies scheming took place in the closed room at night. The guards and prisoners always were attempting to gain advantage over one another but definite limits of behavior seem to be the rule of the conduct of both parties.

On perhaps a hundred occasions we had to be counted two or three times while standing in formation (I remember the cold days). A few times, after roll call outside, we were sent back to our rooms only to be recalled an hour later. About once every two weeks, despite all the German efforts, they could not get the camp count to come out correctly. In that case the guards would have to count the men in each room at night. This procedure was called a picture parade, which, I previously described.

The twice daily Prisoner Of War count was the key to German control and knowledge of camp activities. An individual escape would show up by this means. It also had value to the Senior American Officers because it was a daily check on each man as to his status, such as sick, missing, in the cooler (solitary confinement), or in the hospital.

During the long hours in camp, one thread of hope kept a person going, and that was the war would soon end. We all knew it would end in the defeat of Germany, but the question in our minds was how it would end, would they kill us, would the allies bomb us by mistake, or just what would happen? The horror stories made public following the war were common knowledge to the prisoners during the war because Kriegies were shifted and shuttled back and forth between camps and some of the prisoners had actually been assigned to work in the German concentration camps. Based on these facts, we knew the Germans had few qualms about killing a few thousand men in Stalag Luft I.

As regards the self education program in prison camp, a few examples were that in each compound classes in teaching the German, French, and Russian languages were held daily, the architects held classes each day in certain rooms on basic drawing and basic architecture, many of the navigators held classes in astronomy at night, there were classes in English, algebra, calculus, trigonometry, religion, etc. held daily in various rooms.

The conduct between the German guards and the individual Kriegies was always interesting. In addition to the inherent duties and obligations of any guard or the prisoners, there was a fine line of acting or role playing. There was a psychological or emotional limit to which each would, or could, go without causing any problems. These limits many times became as fine as the edge of a razor. These limits or behaviors were being tested all the time in many subtle ways, such as trading cigarettes for extra shower water, which was forbidden by the German rules in camp, demanding another lump of coal for the room, bribing the guard for cigarette lighter fluid (kerosene was very difficult to use, but was acceptable for a Kriegie), becoming too friendly with the guards, complaining about the camp regulations with the guards, and making inappropriate remarks about the war and the way it was going, in favor of the Allies.

In turn, the German guards were desirous of having a group of docile men that would not cause any trouble, so there would be no need for night time roll calls or extensive searches. Perhaps most important to the individual guards would be they did not want any trouble with the POWs which would bring their name to the attention of the commanding officer in a derogatory light. If the German commander did not like a guard, off he would go to the Russian front (death). The German commanders were given monthly quotas of men to fill and send to the Russian front. This was the key to the manner in which the German commandant maintained very strict discipline over his guards and the reason they would do exactly what he said. When a guard was walking across a compound and a German officer called his name, he "froze in his tracks" until given further instructions from the officer.

Through the thoughts and daily life of the Kriegies, self education played a part. Every man thought of the day he would be arriving at home and he wanted to return home a better man than when he left the States. The prisoners represented a rough cross section of middle class America and education had been always spoken of in the home and in the school as a sure way to success. The great depression had just ended as these men had enlisted or been drafted into the Air Force and education had been the principal part of all their years. Most of the prisoners came from what would be called poor families. However, all families were poor in the 1930s in the United States. The Kriegies were men who had, so far, made it financially. In the Air Force they were paid approximately three times what an ordinary job would pay in civilian life and they were determined not to let this success slip out of their grasp.

The Air Corps, in all their tests, evaluation, and assignments, stressed education. It was easier, for example, to receive pilot training with some college. This is not to say there are not men with an 8th grade education who could not fly as good, if not better, than a college graduate. To fly you need more than a diploma.

Whenever a group of persons of one sex gather there comes up the question of homosexual activity, that is, when they are confined for a long period of time in close quarters. I can never recall any homosexual activity in the prison camp and I cannot recall any talk or rumors of such activities in the camp. This is not to say these activities did not play a part in the lives of some of the men, but in all honesty I could say it was at a much more reduced level than one would find in a normal society.

Lice control program

In a large P.O.W. Camp such as Stalag Luft I, the German Commander and the American Senior Officers were concerned about epidemics breaking out among the men.

Lice, body bugs and other crawling insects posed a problem. One method of control was to wash all the hairy parts of your body once a month in kerosene. A small can of kerosene with a little rag was passed from room to room. First a scissors would be passed around and all the hair cut short and then washed with the kerosene rag.

This procedure was good for a few laughs as some Kriegie would cut a little too close or the kerosene would burn and the P.O.W. would cuss the Germans, the lice and the war. His buddies would offer no sympathy, only remarks about his own stupidity.

Shower parade

The term "shower parade" was used when a group of 100 Kriegies were given the opportunity to take a shower. The frequency was irregular; when I first arrived at camp we were given a shower once every two weeks; during 1945 this frequency dropped to about once in six weeks.

The Germans would take us, barracks by barracks, and we would be called out and marched to the shower building just outside our compound. The American senior officers would call the men and actually get them into a formation.

The shower procedure reminded one of a "Marx Comedy" or the "Three Stooges". When we arrived in the building, the shower heads were in the center of the room, perhaps 25, the clothes were taken off and piled around the room on some wooden benches.

With everyone ready the shower master who controlled the water shouted something in German and the Kriegies yelled, "Here she comes!" In about 5 or 10 seconds the water stopped and all the men lathered up with soap. The first time the water was cold so the Kriegies jumped around and cussed the German shower master.

At about this time, some POWs who could speak German approached the shower master and asked if he would run warm water for 10 seconds. The German turned this request down and yelled something in German and down would come the torrent of water for 5 seconds. The Kriegies all remained standing and the Kriegie asked for 10 more seconds of warm water and offered a cigarette in exchange.

I noted the shower master at this point would give in, usually, and as he slipped the cigarette into a little hiding place in his little office he would turn on the warm water for 15 seconds leaving everyone happy.

During the winter months when showers were available, perhaps once a month, as many as 25% of the Kriegies would not take a shower. This going to the shower building took extra effort and the POWs had adjusted to living without bathing. Occasionally on a warm day some of the men would take a sponge bath on the south side of the barracks.

Air raids

When I was in the camp, we had air raids, many in the day time, and always at night. As a Prisoner of War, there is nothing in the world a prisoner can do when the air raid sirens go off. The civilian population would go to shelters, but not us. We would run inside if it was day light, and if at night, the lights would go out at once. The Air Raid sirens made an interesting sound like a giant musical symphony playing in the night. The sounds varied each night during each air raid and were, to a large extent, dependent upon the wind and the weather.

In addition, there would be minute variations in the sound of each siren, then the raid would come from various directions during the night, and sometimes there would be multiple raids so the sirens would set up their wail from various directions.

To understand the air raid siren set-up, you must know the sirens were set up all over Germany and they apparently were activated by a master control network. As a fleet of bombers or night fighters approached, the sirens would start screaming in front and to the right and left of the probable bomber path. The sirens wailed in a fan-like shape that extended about 75 miles ahead of the actual bomber trace. Consequently, various sirens were starting to sound and others were dying out as this great symphony was taking place. Then, as a climax to these sounds, we would hear the bombs drop and hear the German fighters bore and buzz their way into the sky. Soon the sirens would die out as the Allied bombers and fighters made their way into new territories or turned towards home.

Usually we were in bed at night and as we heard the sirens wail we could reasonably well determine what cities were being bombed. We became so sophisticated in analyzing the situation that we gave names to the British fighters that would make certain passes at night. Our hero was the fighter bomber that would, about three times a night, fly into Berlin at tree top level and drop a 2,000 pound bomb right on the center of the city. He came in so low they could not shoot him down. If they did, his buddy would replace him and would be there in a few hours. This was psychological warfare in its ultimate form. That is, not much damage except harassment of millions of people every night.

When the raids were close to the camp in the day time or night time we would look for the planes and cheer our buddies on. This would sometimes take the form of opening a window at night and calling out "Come on, Bombers". In the day time we would see the planes and watch the fighters attacking the planes. At night we saw the anti aircraft fire firing their long tracer bullets into the sky, and, in addition, we could see the German fighters firing at the bombers in the sky. These were dramatic and I always noted it seemed at night there was always an added drama because you could see and hear much more than in the day time.

Also, at night, when the anti-aircraft fire struck a bomber and it exploded in the air, it resulted in much more dramatic sight than when a bomber was shot down or exploded in the daytime. Anybody can visualize a bomber exploding in the day time, but the colors and the slowly falling debris make a spectacular sight at night. Occasionally a fighter would get shot down but it did not put on much of a show.

The most spectacular sight I have ever witnessed was the bombing of a large oil refinery near Barth, Germany on about 15 March 1945. This was a large oil storage and refinery complex located between Stettin, Germany and our prison camp at Barth. It was a clear, cold night when the air raid sirens began their mournful wail, and within a few minutes we knew the action would be up in our section of Germany. Within the next minutes, a couple of low flying British Mosquito bombers passed near by; in their path, the 88mm anti-aircraft shells could be seen leaving a trail of light. The German light anti-aircraft guns with their tracer bullets, wove a web of crisscross lights through the clear night air. Then much to our astonishment, one of the bombers began dropping white flares at about 5,000 feet around the oil refinery target. This circle was about 10 miles in diameter. Within seconds followed two more light British bombers that flew at about 2,500 feet, dropping a series of green flares at intervals of about 2,000 feet in a 3 mile diameter circle. Now there were two gigantic circles hanging in the sky. Then in seconds two more fighter bombers came in at about a 1,000 feet and flew a tight circle about one mile across, and dropped red flares at about 1,000 feet. The concentric rings in the sky had set the stage and set up the target area for the Royal Air Force bombers.

Just after the panorama of color circles had been set up, the first plane in a string of about 1,500 British four engine bombers began to hit the drop point in the sky. By now the German big 88mm guns had started to throw up the curtains of anti-aircraft fire. As each shell reached its height of about 25,000 feet, it exploded in a multicolored yellow, red, and white explosion. The anti-aircraft search lights were stabbing and searching the sky. In the next few seconds, the first of the 1,000 pound bombs slammed into the refinery. The roar in the sky had turned into constant rumble; the fire on the ground was so constant that the individual shells being fired tended to blend together.

The program had begun—men, machines, lights, and sound. In a few moments we were to see the results of a bomber being hit directly by an 88mm shell. The bomber, its bombs, and thousands of gallons of high test gasoline erupted in a giant ball of fire, going thousands of feet in the air. Then the individual parts of the plane still burning rained down as if it were a fire spurt from a garden hose. Some parts burned until they hit the ground, while others vanished in the black clear night. Then a bomber would be hit and start down, trailing a long plume of fire. Gradually its speed would increase and soon it would be headed straight down. In moments there would be a big explosion as it hit the ground. A tremendous explosion and then a giant ball of flame, and then everything seemed quiet as the flame died down and our attention was drawn to other action. Some bombers, when hit, would go into a long glide and disappear over the horizon only to appear again as a ball of flame in the distance.

The flares of various colors still hung in the sky but they were no longer needed by the bombers in locating the target. The oil refinery was by now burning. Every few seconds thousands of pounds of high explosive would hit the refinery. The most dramatic events of the night would be when a large bomb would strike directly into a huge gasoline tank. A giant ball of colored flame would erupt and obscure momentarily many of the other fires.

Continuously the small caliber guns and the large caliber artillery would be firing a constant stream of shells into the sky. Occasionally, from the shell explosions and from the search lights, we would catch sight of the bomber stream. It kept coming in an endless stream and there was nothing in the world that could stop it. Tonight about 40 large four engine Lancaster bombers were shot down on this raid. Once in a while we would catch a fleeting glimpse of a parachute hanging in the sky.

By now the German fighters would be up in full strength and you could hear the high pitched whine of the motors and occasionally see the burst of their machine gun fire. As part of the plan, more light bombers came in at this time and illuminated and pinpointed the target for the bombers. The bomber stream was hundreds of miles long and would go on until the last bomber dropped his load of bombs. As the fighting increased, the fighters and anti-aircraft fire occasionally would find a cripple and all hell would descend on this poor guy. If he was crippled his altitude would fall, his speed decrease, and he would become more vulnerable. Sometimes they would get him and sometimes they would fail.

This giant spectacle was played out over a number of miles in all directions from the refinery and up to six miles high. The air was constantly being fanned by the tracer bullets from the ground, along with the searchlights. I thought to myself, if only someone had a camera to record this spectacular event because it could never be recreated in a motion picture and perhaps would never be played out in real life, or war, again.

Gradually, after about 90 minutes, the show began to slow down. Fortunately we had a window that opened on the scene. In addition, that night, we had a mirage in the area. The air was clear and still so that the sounds would come through in a true sound wave pattern. We Kriegies had been crowded around the open window and had strained to observe and listen to the sight. When it was over, we were very tired. The raid had taken place between one and three in the morning. There could not have been much left of the storage and refinery area when the raid was over.

An event such as this made the guards very nervous the next morning. We were usually a little cautious in making any cutting remarks. They would perhaps be reserved to such remarks as "Did you see the show last night?", "You're lucky you have horses in camp to carry supplies", "Did you sleep well last night?", etc. There were other raids too but not as dramatic. The other large raids were by the

American Air Force on the Stettin, and the Penemünde area in the daylight bombing of the German missile complex.

War closes in on camp

With the air raid sirens every day wailing for perhaps an hour or two, and with the night raids lasting several hours, the war always seemed close at hand. Every day you could hear anti-aircraft fire, and planes flying in combat, but soon the war was going to take on a much closer complexion. Soon we were going to hear the rumble of the Russian artillery as it literally chewed up everything in its path in its drive into East Germany and the total destruction of Germany and its culture.

During the fall and winter, almost every room had its map of the war zone. The maps were drawn with great detail and great care. With our overall information, we could pinpoint the Russian front and the Allied front in detail. With our information we could also pinpoint the salient points on both fronts and measure the progress daily. It soon became apparent the Russian Armies would come to liberate our camp. These maps were kept hidden from the Germans.

Daily the news became more tension filled as we estimated the Russians to be only about 125 miles to the southeast. Then early one morning, an officer rushed into our room and stated the Russians were coming. This moment is bell clear in my mind. Sure enough, when we opened our window, we could hear the steady rumble of the artillery from the east. This barrage lasted about four hours. Could it be they had bypassed Stettin, 125 miles to the southeast? Could it be that sound could carry so clearly for over 100 miles? Soon things became quiet, and there was nothing to do but await the evening "POW WOW" newspaper. Our hopes were shattered when it gave an account of the shelling of Stettin. The Russians were still a long ways away, perhaps 125 miles.

From that day in early April until we were liberated in May, we were able to discern artillery fire almost every day. The volume and loudness of the sound was, to a large extent, determined by the atmospheric conditions.

The time was growing tense. Every man had deep serious thoughts within himself as to how he would end up. Would he be taken hostage by the Germans? Would they, in desperation, just kill us? Perhaps they would move our camp? Perhaps the Russians would not know of our status and would bomb the Camp? As the major cities, armies, and areas of Germany were falling, it became apparent we were in a unique position. Maybe we were the last great hope and asset the Germans had left? They had many other prison camps, but none as large, and none in the position that it could be used as a bargaining item. The British and the United States Armies were moving ever eastward and the Russian Armies from the east were moving westward. Somewhere, sometime, somehow, there would be an end, someway.

Being on the extreme north flank of the final remnant of Germany presented us with a unique opportunity to witness the death of a nation. To hear, in the daytime, the relentless pounding of the Russian artillery, and to see, at night, the stabbing glow of the Russian artillery as it moved westward—regardless of a man's limited view of history, one could sense through his eyes and ears, the writing of another chapter in European history. Russian Armies do not march across the face of Europe for training or show.

The air war was also being brought into focus by the view of almost constant contrails in the air representing enemy and friendly planes. The air raid sirens wailed their mournful funeral sound as they tried desperately to follow the action. Now the action was getting ahead of the sirens and about all they could do was to scream in unison as the action enveloped them. The planes would bomb or strafe and then the sirens would start. They were like old men—the action has passed them by.

It was interesting as an Air Force officer to realize, in the final analysis, what happened in the air or on the sea had little to do directly with the march of the armies on the ground. In the final battles the airplanes were on the ground and the air was quiet as the men on the ground fought and took the final miles of German soil. As the planes and armies of Germany were being cut to pieces, the last miles of Germany were being defended with a form of fanaticism that is unknown to the average man or soldier. Death itself was meaningless. The only thing that had any value was the Father Land. Strange, final days of German resistance would be the effort and will of teenage, fanatic children.

During the last weeks of the war it became known to the camp and the Kriegies that the American Air Force was aware of our plight. As the war moved into its final days, the United States was actively putting together a special force that would help the Prisoners of War. This would take the shape of a parachute division—hundreds of transport planes, glider troops, and other airborne units. During the last weeks of the war, the United States actively recaptured two American

Prisoner of War camps by utilizing Army and Air Force troops. These camps, however, were small and it was done as a protective and preventative measure rather than any overt military action.

The word Russian (to the Germans) was the worst word in their language. In talking to the German guards, the Kriegies who were masters at needling the Germans, would invariably bring up the subject of the Ruskies. This was our word we used when talking to the guards about the Russians. I can recall on several occasions we would tell the guard something about the Ruskies and his face would turn white and he would tremble at our story. He knew we were perhaps lying, but he could not help himself.

By now it looked as if the Russians would overrun our camp and it was a foregone conclusion the Russians would kill all the guards. As the panorama of war unfolded before our eyes, our prophecy proved to be correct. The day would someday come when the guards would crawl on their hands and knees up to us, asking for mercy, forgiveness, and life itself.

So-called "odd balls" would come into camp from various sectors of the war zones. For example, American officers who had, for some reason or another, ended up on a labor gang in Poland. Whenever one of these strangers came to camp I made it a point to visit them and listen to the stories they had to tell. One British officer had ended up in Poland with a gang of Jewish women on a railroad rebuilding gang. The Germans were determined to use these women to the ultimate and then to let them die. On the gang he was with three hundred Jewish women who were housed in a barn-like structure. The Germans issued one loaf of black bread for every ten women and then required them to go out and work all day. Gradually they became thinner and thinner. They were beaten with whips to keep them going. He thought women were outstanding in their stamina and said they would work until they dropped and then the other women would dig a shallow hole along the tracks and bury the dead women at the end of the day. It was beyond my self respect to ask if the German guards took advantage of the women in any other way and he did not volunteer the information.

One of the most horrible stories of the war was told by an American Air Force officer who somehow had gotten himself into a German hospital in Berlin. This was during the closing months of the war. This hospital in Berlin acted as a terminus for the railway hospital trains coming from the Russian-German front. There were many hospitals, but this was the main one.

This officer worked in the receiving section of the unit. When a train arrived the box cars were opened and he was one of those men who sorted out the dead from the living. Those that were living, were in turn, sorted out as to who might live and those not expected to live. The wounded would then be wheeled to the operating rooms and the dead would be consolidated into one box car and shipped on out of the city. After the train had departed, he was detailed to remove the amputated arms and legs from the operating room into a basement room. The rags, paper, etc. were burned in open incinerators, but the legs and arms (especially the legs) were just tossed into a basement room. No one ever expected they would be cleaned out of the room, because everybody lived from day to day. As the Russians arrived, he and all members of the staff and workers left the hospital as individuals and struck out for themselves. By some fortune or fate, he was assigned the barracks in which I lived.

This young officer who had worked in the German hospital in Berlin stated the only hope the Germans had was for the American Armies to join the German Army and start fighting against the Russian Armies in the central part of Germany. He said 100% of the Germans would then side with the Americans and would ultimately repel the Russians from the Father Land. I cited the above statement as the work of one man, but this idea had been imbued into the German minds during the last few months of the war. Many German units in the field took on an air of victory as they waited to join forces with the Allied armies and send the Russians back to the steppes of Russia. They hated, feared, and cursed any information or mention of the Russians Armies. The Germans did not have this attitude toward the Americans, whom they considered only pawns in the world game of war and Judaism or Semitism.

An interesting note in the battle casualties in the last couple of months of the war on the Eastern Front (Russia) was that many of the men dressed in German Army uniforms were not Germans. They were foreign kids who had been recruited in lands taken over. It was estimated 90% of the dead and injured arriving in the Berlin hospital during the last month of the war were not of German extraction. This was in accordance with some overall scheme to save the German young people and German blood on which to build a new Germany. This may sound odd or unrealistic, but many aspects of war are not very practical. The defeats and victories are known for several months before the white flags have their day of surrender. The peasants fight and the General's plan. The peasants die, the Generals live. The peasants march, and the Generals rest. War seems so stupid to everyone, but men always look ahead for something better.

Germany is dying

29 April 1945.

The Russians are advancing closer. The tank barricades in Barth are being torn down and evacuation of women and children has started. The word is that some of the German Storm Troopers are leaving. The Prison Camp is still officially in German hands. Everyone is very tense.

The Russians should be here very soon. German soldiers are changing uniforms for civilian clothes in Barth. Henry "The Butcher" is reported dead. He was reported found in a butcher shop cut up into the normal hog cuts and hanging on hooks in the shop. This thought filled the normal "Kriegie" with a satisfied feeling, because Henry was mean in a real and true sense that cannot be conceived by normal persons.

The rumor is now the German guards in camp have started to leave. There is a question if the roll call in the evening will be called by the Germans or the Americans. The officials in camp here today instructed us to dig trenches to protect ourselves in case of air raids. The question now is whether this is an American camp, in charge of Colonel Zemke? Late in the afternoon Russian POW figures or letters were painted on the roofs of some of the barracks in an attempt to save ourselves from bombing attacks.

Tension is very high at all times. Everyone is listening for artillery shells that may soon be falling within a few miles of camp. The few Germans remaining state the artillery is German bombing of the Russian front lines. The German soldiers are now spreading the rumor that the German officers will be deserting their soldiers within the next few hours. All the German officers are drunk.

As I went back to my little room to write the above words I had the overpowering feeling I was a part of history and it was taking place within sight and sound of my very being. Yet nothing important seemed to be happening. The hours slowly moved by. Late in the afternoon we are called out for roll call. The German guard who counted our block was again crying and very dejected. I tried to console him but his world was rapidly coming to an end and he knew it better than I. Towards dusk the Russian artillery started up within about ten miles. A few sirens made their last feeble wails, the acrid fumes of shells and rumble of explosions now filled our eyes and ears. Every hour was now important, the rumors flew, and we felt the end was very near. How would it end? When would it end? As I lay down on my thin mattress bed, it was hard to relax. Something could happen any hour, and I wanted to be in on the event.

30 April 1945.

The day breaks grey and cold. Tension is high. In the morning the Germans start demolition activity. The anti-aircraft school is the first building to go. Fires start at various German military installations in the area. The blue and light brown smoke slowly drifts over the camp from the explosions and fires. Russians are now reported ten miles from the camp and marching closer. Civilians can now be seen on the roads, moving away from Barth towards the west, away from the Russians. Everything is now confusion.

A few German guards are around camp but they have moved from their quarters into one of the empty barracks in our compound. They looked like a sorry lot of defeated men. We now start learning about the hundreds of German atrocities that have occurred in the Barth area. German guards have now started leaving. The Germans say the war is "kaput". The word is that the last of the German personnel in camp will be leaving at 10.30 in the evening. As night falls, Russian artillery lights up the sky to the south and east. In Barth you could hear people screaming, and the few trucks, cars, and horse drawn wagons were leaving the area.

A most interesting note that I paid particular attention to was the dogs seemed to sense something was wrong before people actually made a move. For the past few hours the dogs have barked incessantly, and I noted after a few hours of barking I would hear the report of a rifle and the barking would stop. Finally tonight, as the light mist and a gentle wind were blowing, I heard the last of the dogs bark and then the yelling of human voices took over the scene. As the human voices screamed, it was apparent the German Empire was falling in one great big heap. It all seemed so dramatic, with the cool air, and the light rain. It was now the 30th of April and we all wondered how it could go on much longer, It was just a matter of hours. Tonight the newspaper did not come out for the first time. It was clear tonight that the Germans would leave and we would have our own camp. Many events lie ahead.

The night Germany fell, April 30, 1945, a victim of the Allied armies of the free world, the last official German Army communiqué was broadcast and heard over the prison camp radio. It stated something everyone should remember: it is quoted in full and true context below.

The news broadcaster was drunk and crying and the following statement represented his official news broadcast and what he, in his heart, felt. It is difficult to determine where the official announcement ends and his heart begins:

"Tonight the outward appearance of a mighty German Reich is falling. Our beloved Fuehrer died a few minutes ago in Berlin, fighting against the Bolsheviks. Berlin is falling. Remember the Rhine and the Oder will always be German Rivers. Remember also they may take our food, our homes, our clothing, but there will always be our Beloved German language that they cannot take from us and upon which we will build another mighty empire. May God spare us."

The German National Anthem was then played for the last time and in a few minutes there was static. Shortly thereafter all was quiet and the last of the German voices fell silent. It was now near midnight. The distant rumble continued and tiny flashes on the horizon in various directions continued. Time had run its course, a chapter in history was being closed, and in everyone's mind there was but one question. What would morning bring?

Stalag Luft I liberated by the Russians

1 May 1945:

This morning the camp is in American hands. No Germans are around in the camp. However, German military personnel and German civilians are now coming to the fence and asking for protection and asking to surrender to the Americans. The Russians are now reported 3,000 yards from the camp with their leading ground elements.

The day passes slowly and we are looking constantly for the Russian Army. In the late afternoon the sirens finally gave up the "ghost" and the fighters and bombers have left. The air is quiet, but the ground is alive with bombs and smoke and small fires.

At 0810 p.m. German standard time I went to a south window of our little room (the only window) to watch the Russian artillery put on a display to the south. A few miles to the south they had apparently run into a German strong point and they were in the process of removing it. At 0835 p.m. I heard a scream in the far end of the camp. My ears perked up; something was happening. The screams turned to a rumble and grew larger and closer. Like a large wave, it was engulfing the camp and within seconds the noise was within a hundred yards and the, above the noise, I heard my dream, "Joe is here". The piercing screams of a few officers came through clearly above the screams of the others. The officer standing next to me jumped through the window after I had yelled "Joe is here". Everyone screamed at the top of their voice.

In seconds, all the Kriegies were outside, yelling and running in a mass towards the origin of the sound. Mass hysteria had overtaken 10,000 men; the individuals mind but a blur, his body super active, he stood and jumped and screamed, his arms were waving, tears flowed down his face. The "Kriegie" had lost all control of mind and body. His physical body was attempting to get rid of the tension.

This was now a mob. Laughter, screams, prayers, and wild eyes were all mixed up in every individual. Hundreds of men ran towards the direction of the origin of the sound and consequently, some ran into barbed wire fences and were cut up and bleeding. This made no difference to the injured men or to the others looking at them with blood running down their arms or face. Each man was in a world by himself and did not care.

As a commentary and after-thought on the liberation celebration, I had an evening of emotional experiences I never had before and will never have again. First, when the word or the screaming reached by ears that "Joe is here", I immediately let go emotionally. I became very excited, very tense physically. I felt nothing was beyond my physical ability. My mind started jumping from one thought to the next, and the words and sentences I spoke became terse and meaningless. Physically I could not remain still. My legs and arms started moving.

I noted exactly the same emotional and physical excitement in the other Kriegies. I felt as if I were no longer an individual but a part of everyone. I was moving in a state of euphoria. I was doing things which were completely out of context with my personality and character. When I yelled and jumped up and down it seemed to be the normal thing to do. The little voice far back in my mind that advised me my actions were strange, was suddenly stilled. I felt I was now my real self, I felt confident I was willing to do anything anyone asked, and they, in turn, would do anything I asked of them. What a wonderful, strange feeling, and I thought, this is the way I will always live.

The strange Kriegies I had known only by sight suddenly turned into bosom buddies. As it was now dusk outside, however, I could see the Kriegies darting back and forth between groups of excited men and various barracks with little meaning except the happiness they were expounding and receiving from all the other POWs in camp.

We were no longer Kriegies, we were free men, on our way to the "land of the big PX" (Post Exchange). As I ran from place to place in the compound, looking up old friends, I began to sense I was not myself, but was a part of a mob. My actions now became predicated on what others were doing. If someone laughed, I laughed. If someone ran, I ran. If I laughed, the others laughed. If I jumped, the others jumped. After about an hour of helter skelter activity, we unconsciously drifted towards the actions of an organized mob. We started moving into a large group and the strains of singing could be heard. At this time, someone thought of the idea of lighting a bonfire in the center of the camp. The fire was started. That was it. We all ran towards the fire and started dancing and singing at the leaping flames.

This was the key. The giant bonfire electrified the prisoners. Their eyes widened; here was the symbol they craved, here was an idol, here was the cause, here was freedom. We had been venting our emotions towards one another, but now we could vent our emotions in fire. What a wonderful symbol, colorful, alive, destructive, beautiful, talking to us with a crackling sound. As the voice of the fire turned to smoke it rose rapidly, straight up into the dark heavens.

The Kriegies ran back to the barracks and started bringing objects of oppression they wished burned, such as the window shutters used during air raids, and posts from the guard fence. As the men returned, they ran towards the fire and they were giving an offering to a God. The flames were devouring the objects with the growing and glowing flames. The prisoners screamed and yelled as each strange object was piled into the sacrificial fire. The ultimate of sacrifice were those objects which had physically held us in confinement. The fence posts, stripped of the barbed wire, lit an additional fire in the heart of every man.

As the bonfire burned, the Kriegies formed circles around the fire, first one, then two, and then three giant circles about 100 feet in diameter, the circles separated by about 10 foot intervals and moving in opposite directions. We were snake dancing. Snake dancing is the ultimate in physical happiness for men. By snake dancing I mean each man held onto the hips of the man ahead and you moved in a swaying, surging, movement that moved around and around the bonfire. Not fast, but keeping step to the singing. The singing was confused, but remarkably in unison as they sang the old songs of the 30s and the early 40s. I recall one of the songs was the "Beer Barrel Polka", and there were many others. Everyone in the compound participated, everyone sang, everyone danced, this was an organized mob. Everyone loved every minute. This was the way we always wanted to live.

(As an after thought, I would like some day to know how women would act and express themselves under conditions of extreme happiness. I know how men act, feel, look and think, but what would a woman do?)

Time began to lose meaning; this would go on forever. The men, in many ways, seemed to revert back into time thousands of years. They became physical beings and exerted themselves in a physical sense. Perhaps, back deep in the mind of every man, is a sense of strength and power that has long been depressed by civilized society. Here we were acting out something back deep in our minds that had been suppressed for thousands of years, but "tonight I am myself".

There was no question of who wanted to do something. Every man participated eagerly and wholeheartedly. Late in the evening, the ultimate symbol of Kriegie life began to play its part. POWs started tearing down some of the guard or watch towers or what were sometimes called floodlight towers. These were built of long posts set in the ground about 10 feet and extended into the air about 30 feet. When a group of Kriegies had liberated one of these poles, a dozen men would come running, the snake dancing lines would break, and they would run full speed up to the fire and let go and then the long post would sail through the air and land on top of the fire. The Kriegies screamed as the long heavy post hit the fire and the resulting sparks and smoke filled the air. The dancing resumed, more Kriegies went for more posts. I thought to myself, this will continue forever. Why not? It is the logical thing to do.

As the long guard tower poles sailed into the flames, I had the strange feeling I was leaving a way of life and entering a new type of life. I was happy, but I had a few other mixed emotions. Now I would have to compete; now I would have to make decisions; now I would have to love; now I would be responsible; now I was out of the womb of Stalag Luft I and facing a new world. Could I face it? How would people treat me? New frontiers lay ahead and they would be strange.

Around the bonfire the minds and the bodies of the Kriegies began to tire beyond their physical and mental endurance. Kriegies started falling on the ground and lay there in their ecstasy. I did not care. I knew everyone was happy because I was happy. Soon the flames of the fire started dying, the red embers were aglow, the snake dance was slowing down. I stayed as long as I could but my legs were getting wobbly, my mind was tired and I began to feel woozy, as if I were drunk. I was staggering in my mind and body. I found a roommate and we slowly walked towards our barracks. I said nothing and he said nothing. What was there to say? As we moved up the dirt covered incline towards the back door my friend caved in and fell softly to the ground. It was warm outside and it never occurred to me to help him into his room. He passed out happily. I made it to my room. I do not recall if the other men were in the room. I found my bed, laid down, and fell asleep.

The next morning I woke up and looked around. The other Kriegies were in bed and sleeping. Clothes were not taken off in camp so getting up in the morning was simple; when you stepped out of bed you were dressed and ready to go for the day.

The first thing I noticed was I was sore over my whole body, and the other men had lost their voices. It seemed almost normal because my voice was also squeaky and weak. I thought briefly about the night before, about the dancing and the singing. The events of the night before occupied very little of my thinking, because what other way would there be to celebrate a liberation? It all seemed so normal and reasonable. In fact, since being liberated, I have never heard of any other way to celebrate a release from a prison camp than to sing and dance. I cannot recall any Kriegies commenting on the liberation celebration because it seemed so reasonable. What else would, or could, a person do in these strange circumstances? The incident seemed to have been so normal by all concerned.

The victory or liberation party immediately receded into some small part of the mind. All my Kriegie events seemed to be stored in a particular part of my brain that is seldom used.

As I live from year to year, I have a feeling I have tasted and felt happiness; that I have known the time when my mind and body took on characteristics that are strange to my behavior today. Perhaps there are few people who have lived for a few hours in ecstasy. The feeling is etched in my mind.

From Stalag Luft I to France

Early in the morning of the 10th day of May we were finally advised we would be leaving Barth by air to a military camp in France. By this time the large German Airfield located a few miles west of Barth had been cleared of mines and a temporary flight control tower was set into operation.

We gathered up our few possessions in a bag and lined up outside our barracks and then the entire camp started marching towards the field. With 10,000 men, this was a large operation to move out in one day. It was about a three hour march to the German air field and we moved out in an orderly sequence that would put us on the field at approximately the time our group of planes would arrive. Planes started coming in at about 10 o'clock in the morning when the first elements of the camp arrived at the field and it was late afternoon before the last of the "Kriegies" arrived to be picked up in U.S. Air Force bombers. I arrived at the field around noon and we had to wait for about two hours for our evacuation ship to come in. During the waiting period we usually inspected the German Bomber factory that built two engine bombers for the German Air Force. In addition they had a small jet fighter factory. I was interested in the German control tower, the equipment and setup. The operations rooms were very much in disarray, desk drawers were laying on the floor, maps laying all over, the minor items of any value had been taken. A little side light was I noted 80% of the maps laying on the floor covered an area between Barth and Sweden, the implication being many of the last planes and pilots had taken off for Sweden rather than surrender to the Russians.

During the flying of the missions over Europe, one was usually a little doubtful about the accuracy of the bombing or how much damage had been done. However, following our release from Stalag Luft I we were flown out of Barth to an American Air Field in France. During this flight the pilots of the evacuation planes took us on an aerial tour over many of the larger cities of Germany and made a run down the Ruhr River Valley industrial complex.

Much to my surprise the destruction had been complete and the cities lay dead. I did not see a person move or any activity in cities as large as Minneapolis or Chicago. It looked to me as if every building and factory in many of these cities had been completely destroyed. What the bombers did not hit, the ensuing fire finished. In looking at these large cities that lay in complete ruin, it was my opinion it would have been much easier to rebuild the cities out in the country because cleaning up the mess looked like a job that would take forever.

In North One compound we had several hundred British officers who had been captured early in the war. These men had been prisoners of war for about five years and it was interesting to note their mental and physical development into long-term Kriegies. These men had learned the German language, they had by now taken the attitude that prison was a natural way of life. The thing that kept them going was their faith in their home country. They had steeled themselves to the everyday problems of prison life and adjusted emotionally to the German guards. They lived with the German guards almost on a flirtation level and from this banter of "give and take" they derived their strength to keep going.

A very interesting fact was as the war ended and as we were getting ready to evacuate the camp, the old time Kriegies and particularly the British, cried like children. Off hand, it seemed so funny to see men cry when they were being told to leave the camp and get ready to go home. To most men this was a period of happiness, but to the old timers, it was a period of sadness. The officers wept openly toward one another and caressed old friends in tears. No words were spoken, only the strength of their arms and the tears on the faces showed as they parted. To them a way of life was coming to an end. These were their friends. With these men they had suffered, laughed, been beaten, shared their meager rations, and above all, they had placed their trust in these men and always found them strong and friendly. A friend in hardship is far different than a friend in good times. A friend in pain is by far different than a friend in pleasure. A friend in trouble is a friend you can not say good-bye to, because he will always occupy a place in your heart.

Camp Lucky Strike, France

Following the sightseeing trip from Barth to France, which covered many of the destroyed cities of Germany, we arrived in Rheims, France, and landed at an American airfield. There we left the planes and were picked up by trucks and taken to a train at Rheims. The train took us to Camp Lucky Strike, located about four miles from the English Channel on the northwest coast of France. This was, beyond a doubt, the largest tent city in the world. They said there were between 75,000 and 100,000 men in this camp waiting their return to the states. It was at this place we had our first meal since capture and started getting back to normal life. I was assigned to a six-man tent located on such and such a street at such and such a number. We finally found it, and here we lived for about three weeks while we waited for a surface ocean ship to bring us back to New York. This camp was so large they fed about 20,000 men in each of the dining hall tents. The line going to the mess hall was about a half mile long, so when you finished one meal you headed back to the end of the line for the next meal. The food was good, but not too ample, because of the huge crush of people. I can still recall they seemed to have boiled chicken every day that was tainted with gasoline.

A strange thing happened on the day we left camp. It was the first and only time I was sick during my prisoner of war experience. After we left Barth and landed in France some kind soul gave each of us a can of grapefruit juice. The can was colored dark brown or olive drab, about a pint in size, and it looked so innocent. That evening, after I arrived in my tent at Camp Lucky Strike, I opened the can and drank down the contents. It really tasted good. In about 10 minutes my world turned upside down. I felt as if a red hot poker had been shoved down my throat and clear through my body. I recall it was dark outside and the moon was shining. I made it about 20 feet into some tall grass and there I lay for several hours in agony and vomited. Finally I dragged myself back to my tent and was now aware that my body just was not accustomed to the strong juices in the can, consequently, the violent illness. This was my first night out of Stalag Luft I. The next day I was fine, but more careful with food.

Our old crew that had originally left England and had been shot down over Germany finally found each other at Camp Lucky Strike, so it made the stay a little more reasonable. I recall Captain Blackburn, Lt. Orr and myself would, almost every day, take long walks into the countryside, perhaps venturing as far as 10 miles from camp. There were a large number of farms and little villages. We would buy bread in these little towns and then buy onions from the farmers so we had something to eat on these long walks and did not have to "sweat" the long lines at the mess tent. In addition to our visiting the countryside, we walked along the coast and looked over the German coastal emplacements that were still standing about the same as they had a year ago when they were captured or overrun. The weather was nice and we enjoyed these long walks contemplating the future and what we would do and how we would do it.

We also received new clothes at this camp and they had a U.S. Army Quartermaster Shower Company where you could go and get a shower. This so-called shower tent was quite an affair, and we enjoyed it very much.

This Shower Company was operated by the U.S. Quartermaster Corps. As you entered this long tent, the first thing you would do is take off all your clothes, and throw them in a pile. Then you would move into another long tent and here they had hundreds of shower heads, running water, and lots of soap was available. Following this you entered another tent and they gave you new towels. Then you entered another tent and were issued a full set of new clothing. So you came out a new man. If something did not fit, all you had to do was go back through the shower to be outfitted again. I never in my life could have imagined there could be so many clothes in one area. They would, for example, have trousers in large boxes and hundreds of boxes of trousers as far as the eye could see. They must have had a million of everything. If new shoes did not fit, they just threw them away and found another pair. I often wondered what happened to the hundreds of acres of clothing.

Following our return to France, one of the first items was to be questioned by American Air Force Intelligence Officers. This had little to do with the tactical or strategic mission we had been shot down on, because this was now history. They did, however, have a particular interest in the names of certain crew members which had not been accounted for during the war. Consequently, an attempt was made to verify information as to the status of missing crews. The briefing was of a hurried nature because there were thousands of men to be questioned. I cannot recall being able to give any information of value to the debriefing teams.

At Camp Lucky Strike we had an opportunity to write a letter home and send a telegram. The telegram did arrive at Fairdale, but the letters did not arrive until after I arrived.

From Le Havre, France to New York

Following this long period in Camp Lucky Strike we were loaded on personnel carrying trucks that held about 100 persons each and trucked to the City of LeHavre, France. In driving to the dock at Le Havre we were trucked around the city and then to the docks for loading on the Military Passenger ship. In driving around the city on the only road available, one could see the results of aerial and naval bombardment. It seemed not only as if every building had been destroyed but that every brick in every building had been struck. It was an impossibility to tell what had been the downtown area, the industrial area, or the homes and apartments. It was a sea of bricks and timbers. It was unbelievable, even the docks were gone, and the ship we loaded on was docked against a temporary steel floating dock that apparently had been floated to the location from England following the war. If someone had told me the city would someday be rebuilt, I would have said they were crazy, because the job would have been impossible.

The ocean trip back to New York was uneventful. We are well, rested, and took things easy. We passed through a little rough weather, but rough weather has little or no affect on Air Force crew members. I don't believe I could get sick on water, and even during storms at sea, I noticed the Army and Navy men, as well as the Air Force ground crews, would get sick, but I have never heard of an Air Force pilot being sea sick. So I always enjoy being at sea.

We arrived at the famous Barnagate Light Ship early in the morning. I had used this light ship about 75 miles out of New York City on hundreds of occasions as a check point in flying patrols for submarines over the North Atlantic, so I felt at home when we passed the ship early in the morning. It was not too long before the Statue of Liberty came into view, with its emotional impact on any person who has been away from the United States—especially, when he had questioned, in his mind, many times, if he would ever see her again. Soon we were at the berth, and then on a train to Camp Kilmer in New Jersey, to await the troop train to Minneapolis.

Camp Kilmer

We stayed in the barracks at Camp Kilmer for about 24 hours. While in this camp a most unusual little incident happened. While on board ship, returning to the states, there was an Army captain who was in charge of the eating arrangements for the various sections of the ship. Everybody couldn't eat at once, and these eating schedules were managed in certain orders. Upon our arrival at Camp Kilmer this captain was assigned to the bed next to mine. We had a little casual conversation from time to time. However, when the troop train was called for Minneapolis, he stated he was waiting for the troop train for Chicago but would be going to Minneapolis in a few days. Being I had lived in Minnesota for a couple of years, I asked where he was going in Minnesota. He replied he was going beyond there up to North Dakota. This struck a note because North Dakota was my destination too. Then I asked where in North Dakota he was going, and his answer was Grand Forks. Grand Forks was striking near home so I asked exactly where he was going. He then said he was going to a little town by the name of Fairdale, which he was sure I had never heard of; however, that was my home town. I asked what his name was and he said Captain Nugent. He said he was going there to, perhaps, marry a girl. This was my home town, so I was by this time extremely interested in who this girl could be. He said she was an Amundrud girl and that her father ran an implement and hardware business in Fairdale. Since Amundrud was my wife's maiden name, I was almost afraid to ask what her first name was. However, he said Junis. This was my wife's sister. I explained I was married to Junis's sister, Edwina, and I asked him how in the world he had ever gotten up there and how he became acquainted with her.

By now they were giving the last call for the train for the Twin Cities. He rapidly explained he had headed a detachment of Army men at Fairdale, helping with the harvest, in 1943. He had gotten to know Junis quite well and now was interested in getting married and would be going up to Fairdale to determine if he would or would not get married. Incidentally, a few days after I arrived in Fairdale, he came up there for a visit. The marriage never did materialize.

Home and family

Leaving Camp Kilmer, the U.S. Army troop train rolled directly to Fort Snelling, Minnesota. From this point we were on our own. Edwina had been notified from Camp Kilmer I was coming, but I wanted to surprise her so I did not notify her from Ft. Snelling. We were there about 24 hours and then were free to go on our own. I took the train to Grand Forks, arriving at about 6 a.m. Then I took a train to Lakota and then transferred to the branch line which ran up to Edmore.

It was a beautiful warm summer day. It was clear and still. I recall the bouncing ride in the railway coach to Edmore and arrived there around 1 p.m. I went uptown to the telephone office and phoned Edwina that I was in Edmore and waiting. I went back to the Great Northern Railway depot, picked up my barracks bag, and went out in the middle of the street, stood by my barracks bag and waited. Edmore is a very small town and my going out onto the Gravel Street and waiting was not unusual.

As I stood there waiting for Edwina to come from Fairdale, which was 15 miles distance. I could feel the war was just about over. The years, the months, the weeks, the days, the hours, had at last turned to minutes. I perhaps did not conform to the usual dress, with my high boots, and my woolen pants and jacket. I recall I was sweating and warm. The sun was now beating down on the light colored gravel road but here I was, at the end of a long adventure. Within minutes I saw the Dodge turn off the highway and start coming up the main street. They could surely see me and I could see them. Time had finally run out. A thousand times I had thought that this moment would never come, a hundred times I thought I would never come back, but now it was all over. The tension, the tightness, the apprehension, was now flowing out of me like a broken dam. It was all over. The Dodge pulled up close and I saw Edwina and the baby. I was not being reunited with my family—I was being reborn in every sense of the word.

As I moved towards the car the doors flung open. I looked at Edwina and thought to myself, is this the way I had pictured her in my mind during the past couple of years? I was trying to compare my mental picture I had drawn and what I actually saw. My thinking process was too slow. In a moment she was near me and my reasoning was gone. Time stopped, arms, lips and bodies blended into one.

Looking into the car was my daughter, so small and delicate. I was afraid to touch Linda because I might hurt her or she may cry or be afraid of me. These were the two things in life I did not want to do. Linda was not afraid. She like the excitement and smiled and laughed at all the commotion. After getting into the car Edwina passed Linda to me. This was one of the proudest moments of her life. Linda, within a minute, felt at home, and by the time we had reached Fairdale half an hour later, Linda was my daughter and Linda knew it.

On our arrival in Fairdale, normal life rapidly returned. I was no longer obsessed by food and food alone. Now my family began to play the family role, and within a few hours the whole "Kriegie" experience seemed like a dream, far away in distance and time.

I hope that, as a result of the experience, I am a little better husband, a little better parent, and a little better person.

The 9/11

Narrated by Coleman Jacobson, Bombardier,
8th Air Force, 392nd Bomb Group, 579th Bomb Squadron

Edited by Erik Dyreborg

Coleman Jacobson, 1943 is pictured above

9/11, 1944

My 11th mission from the 392nd Bomb Group took place on September 11, 1944. We took off in our B-24 that morning, probably about 6 am, and flew north from The Wash to our assembly point, which was over the North Sea area, just north of Norwich, England. Our assembly was completed about 7:30 or a quarter of 8. I think I Group put up about 36 aircraft in three wings on that particular mission. We joined a larger formation over the English Channel heading northward towards the Initial Point, which was somewhere south of the city of—Hannover was the target area. The Initial Point was somewhere southwest of Hannover at a designation I cannot recall, but we made that area in about three hours flying time, during which we were attacked by fighter planes, somewhat over Germany after we had crossed the border of the Low Lands. I don't remember precisely where it was, but they were German Squadrons with the yellow nose. They probably came from bases in France, I think, at that time.

They did a fair amount of damage on our right outboard engine, which had to be feathered at the time we reached the Initial Point, but we were still flying within the formation and keeping up rather well. So we continued on with our mission.

Around about 11:30 or so, we began to get a considerable amount of FLAK, and we were hit in the inboard engine on the same side that we had lost the outboard engine to fighter attack. At that particular point, we had begun to lose a little altitude, but we were just about in the target area, so we were able to drop our bomb load perhaps around twelve or twelve-thirty in the early afternoon.

At that particular point, we began to lose altitude, and we deviated from the formation somewhat and started to have a great deal of trouble. I personally was not aware of what was going on in the pilot compartment in that I was sitting in the bombardier's seat up in the front of the aircraft, but was suspicious that something was not going well, because we began to slip considerably. And I understood from comments on the interphone that there was some fire in the bomb bay and one of the gunners had been wounded, probably from the FLAK we received between the IP and the target, which was probably around twenty-five and thirty minutes of flying time.

In any event, shortly before 1 o'clock, we got word from the pilot that he was going to order us to abandon the ship, because he didn't feel we could fly across the Channel and make it back. He was not able to anticipate a crash landing.

So the order to Bail Out at liberty was given.

Now being up in the front part of the aircraft, as far as I could recollect, we had to make sure we had our chest pack on, because we did not wear those during the operation. So it was on the floor, somewhere behind us. I can't recall exactly.

But we followed all of the procedures we were taught. We hooked on the chest pack, tightened up our harness, and made sure everything was in order, and started to crawl back on the cat walk to get to the open bomb bay where we could abandon the aircraft.

By the time I got back there, there were still two of the personnel—I couldn't recognize who they were, because there was a lot of confusion and consternation as you can imagine, however everybody seemed to have kept their wits about them and were functioning in the way in which they had been taught. I, in particular, was rather calm and precise about doing what I was supposed to do.

Bailing out

I got to the open part of the bomb bay and went head first out without much thought of anything else, just popped out.

We were probably about 10,000 or 12,000 feet at that point, and while I had been disconnected from oxygen supply for perhaps four or five minutes at that point, I was OK. I could breathe and think fairly clearly as far as I can remember.

After leaving the aircraft, I didn't black out, but I just couldn't remember things for a while. How long the while was is hard to figure, but I imagine I had fallen about a minute or so when I began to realize that I was like an airplane and I could control my position by using my arms and my torso in such a way that I would fall to the left or fall to the right or fall lying on my back looking upward or lying on my stomach looking downward.

So I fell in every one of those positions, but the only one I eschewed was falling head first downward, because somehow or other, it struck me as a not a very good thing to do.

I began to watch the land to see when there was some apparent motion. We were taught that you should not pull your rip chord until you saw relative motion between yourself and the ground. That was, purportedly, between three and five thousand feet.

When I felt I could see relative motion, in other words, the ground was moving up, it wasn't doing it very fast, but it was an appreciable change from what it was at a higher altitude—let's say at 10,000 feet where you didn't have any idea of relative motion in relation to yourself and the earth—however, there were no aircraft around that we could see and there were no explosions that I could see, nor did I see any other parachutes.

So I must have pulled my rip chord at 3 or 4 thousand, probably. It canopied very nicely. I didn't have to use any auxiliary help. I rolled onto my back and pulled the rip chord. The chute canopied nicely. There was a slight jerk, but not bad, and I was in the upright position, in a very still situation.

As a matter of fact, this whole business was still as soon as I left the aircraft and no longer heard the engine noises, it was very, very quiet. It was rather pleasant in a way, they whole sensation of falling. You didn't have any relative motion. It was quiet and pleasant and rather nice to a certain extent. I can see why President Bush wanted to do some more parachuting when he got older.

In any event, it wasn't very long after my parachute canopied, perhaps two or three minutes I would think, that I was on the ground. I landed on the outskirts of a fairly large city—I guess it was Hannover. I don't think I was more than 15 or 18 miles from the city. Perhaps it was further. I had no way of judging except by what happened to me afterwards.

Captured

I landed in a rural type of area, but a house was very close by. This lady was standing on her doorstep that was in the back there, and I landed, not a rough landing, but evidently my left knee had been injured and it was bleeding around there. I first noticed it at the time I hit the ground. I gathered up the parachute. She was yelling. She didn't approach me, but by the time I got the parachute all bundled, a whole crowd of people—well, ten or twelve people—there was a young kid there, he couldn't have been more than ten or twelve years old with—I can't remember if he was with his brother or his father or—he was with an older person. He was yelling and throwing things. I don't know what he was throwing, but I didn't get hit by anything. But I remember him throwing and everybody was yelling.

Somebody was brandishing a pole or a stick of some sort. He came forward yelling and screaming and waving the stick. I can't remember if he hit me with it or he didn't, but it was sort of consternation there for a while. Nobody had any weapons. I didn't have a pistol with me. I don't know what happened to the pistol I usually carried in the aircraft, but I didn't have it on me.

I was probably lucky, because if they had found one on me they might have shot me with it. But in any event, everything happened rather quickly as far as I can recall, but it probably took thirty or forty minutes before some official in a uniform, probably a policeman, came and took charge of me and the situation and got all of the civilians off my back, so to speak, and got me into a truck.

The truck went to some sort of a building where there were two other American airmen whom I didn't know. They were not from our crew. I didn't see anybody from our crew at that point.

These other guys—I don't remember any conversation we had with one another. We were all, I guess frightened or concerned or one thing or another. I frankly can't remember much of our discussion or thinking at that time.

The uniformed man got the three of us together and took us into a police station, I guess, which I guess was one-half maybe three-quarters of an hour away, probably towards that town, which I think was on the outskirts of Hannover, because we wound up in Hannover by that night. I'm talking now about, perhaps, two o'clock in the afternoon, two or three o'clock in the afternoon.

We just sat in that place until it became dark. We were then taken to another place, probably in the city of Hannover at that time, because from this point, there was a collection of quite a number of airmen who had gotten shot down that day. There must have been at least fifteen who were assembled together and taken to the train station, which was a fairly large area. Most of the passengers got onto trains at street level, I guess, but they took us down two or three series of stairs into a basement area or even a sub basement area in which, I don't recall seeing any tracks there although there were tracks one or two levels above that. But this area was then serving as an underground shelter, because the rumor was there was going to be bombing that night, the British were coming over, which they had been doing regularly over the previous few nights, I guess.

By that time, there were milling around there quite a number of people, both military and civilian. There was a lot of glowering towards us and mutterings of one type or another, which is an uncomfortable situation, as you can imagine.

In any event, the bombing probably started—I would guess it was probably ten or eleven o'clock at night by then. I lost track of time, but quite a bit had gone by and seemed to be going pretty fast as far as we were concerned or I was concerned anyhow.

Being in an area that was being bombed was not a very pleasant situation, I can tell you. The noise was hellacious, the rattling of the building and glass exploding and one thing or another. It was uncomfortable deal all around.

We sort of took a very low profile, as you can imagine. We said very little. We kept out of the way, so to speak.

This all lasted less than an hour, probably, and then it was quiet again. Then we were marched up to the top and assembled into a larger group. There must have been at least twenty people there.

Train ride to the interrogation center

We were put on a train. It wasn't a bad train, actually. There were two or three guards on either side of the train in this one compartment we were in.

The train took off. They didn't feed us anything. We didn't have anything to eat. I don't know if anybody was smoking or not. They may have if they had any cigarettes.

Nobody said much. There wasn't hardly any conversation either between the Americans or the German guards. Probably by the time that train took out of that station, it was probably midnight and maybe even later, because it was daylight by the time we got to where we were going, which as I recall was probably a place called Wetzlar.

We got off the train and were taken to a building. Here again, I can't remember any details except that I remember giving my name, rank, and serial number and that's all.

And we were put into a solitary confinement situation. I don't remember much else that went on is Wetzlar or how long we were there—probably a couple of days, anyhow. There was no conversation between me and any of the other POWs at that point.

Then we were all assembled again and marched out and put on another train which took us to the marshalling yards in Frankfurt-am-Main, the big Frankfurt.

From there we were assembled into a larger group—might have been thirty or forty, and we were marched from the railroad station to, as I recall, we were put on a trolley car or something similar to a trolley car, maybe an interurban. It wasn't a regular train.

The interrogation center

We got off at a place called Oberursel, which was up, it was elevated. It was not a mountain, but a hilly type of a place. At that point, we were taken off that rail car and marched up a hill to a trolley, a streetcar they put us on and took us to this building which said Taunus. Here was a kind of a large facility which had individual rooms, I guess, because I was put into a room by myself. It was a small room about 8 X 10 floor space, maybe less, with a bed in it. And that's all. There was nothing on the wall that I can recall. Some people had marked some marks like you make four strokes and one stroke through them to make it five, kind of indicating that this was the number of days that somebody was there.

I figured I was going to be there for a while and probably was. I don't remember how long I was there, but I don't think it was more than three or four days.

I was getting some food a couple of times a day—like bread and coffee—something, maybe some vegetables. Other than that, I don't remember.

I was taken out to the bathroom, to the toilet, whenever I banged on the door. One time, in the hall, I saw this American who looked terrible. He hadn't shaved in a week, at least, and his hair was all disheveled. His face and upper abdomen had some injuries. It wasn't bleeding, but he had a lot of crusting on his face, and with what was probably five or six days of beard, he looked dreadful.

He didn't say anything to me—just met him in the hall while he was being led by somebody else. I subsequently met this guy in the Prison Camp. His name was Major Mozart Kaufman. I found out later that he had been shot down in his fighter plane. Actually, he was injured by his own bomb. They told me he was strafing and the bomb fell out of the aircraft and exploded underneath him and damaged his plane. He was able to get enough elevation to get out of the airplane, but he was banged up quite a bit. Nothing terribly serious, I don't think, but anyways covered with bleeding. He was bloody. By the time I saw him, he had a lot of scabs and crusts and his face looked terrible. Although we found out he wasn't cut as severely as it looked.

That gave me a lot of food for thought, because he was the first guy I saw at this prison camp that was in bad shape. I didn't know, at that time, whether he something had happened to him, whether they were beating him up or torturing him, or what. It was just that all these thoughts went through your head and you couldn't reconcile them at that point.

I don't recall that they even interrogated me at that place, except maybe once, they took me to a room and offered me a cigarette and asked me what Bomb Group I was with and where I came from. I didn't tell them that, I just gave them my name, rank, and serial number. But they didn't bother with me very much. I don't think I was there fifteen minutes and they put me back in my little room.

I imagine it was less than five days that I was there—probably three or four days.

Train ride to camp

They got me out one morning. A whole bunch of us out and took us, marched us to the train station, where—again I'm a little bit fuzzy whether they took us from there by train. I don't think we went on that trolley car, but they took us to some sort of an urban—we probably went to some sort of a collection point outside the Frankfurt marshalling yards, but not terribly far away.

Evidently there were a lot of POWs they had grouped there over the past week or so, because we made up a train that we later found out was up north to probably Frankfurt am Oder, which one of the places I remember seeing from the train. That took three or four days, I think, to get there.

In between, we stopped a lot on that train. There were quite a few POWs on that train, but there wasn't a lot of conversation between the POWs. People would ask others for a cigarette or something like that, but there was no conversation about who you were or where you came from. There was nothing of that sort.

The guards were none descript. They were older people and they weren't nasty or mean or pleasant. They were just none descript.

We were abandoned a couple of times because of air raids. We were put off on sidings and left there for a while. As I recall, the toilet facilities on these cars were kind of messy. They were there so we had a place to go when we needed to.

They didn't feed us on the train, but periodically, the train would stop and they would have food there. They would have soup, they had boiling pots of soup and some bread and some vegetables—rutabagas and potatoes, nothing very substantial, but something.

Time went slowly. It probably took three days before we got to where we were going, which subsequently we found out was Stalag Luft I in Barth, Germany. It was in the northern part of Germany on the Baltic Sea. It bordered on the Baltic Sea. On a clear day, you could see the Danish coast from the camp.

Camp life in Stalag Luft I

It was kind of a marshy area. There were a lot of birds there. I remember seeing large water fowl, large birds, we could see on the beaches or off shore, particularly if they had nesting grounds in that area. That is one the impressions I got there, that there were a lot of birds.

We were taken off the train and marched to this prison camp. And like typical Americans, there were the prisoners who were already there were all congregating around to watch the fresh new blood being brought in there. They were all yelling out things like, "Oh boy, you'll be sorry." "You won't like it here." And then others would yell out, "Hey, what's happening back in the base 392?" "Do you know so and so?" "What have you heard about this and that?"

Everybody there was looking for news, whatever news we could bring to them.

We didn't know what was going on there, and somehow or other, these things didn't make a lot of sense to us. However, after the initial business of getting accommodated, we were all taken into the prison camp and assigned to new quarters.

I was assigned to Barracks 209. The Barracks Leaders in that particular barracks I knew very well up until this day. They were W. T. Jones from Goose Creek, Texas. He and Dusty Rhodes had a two man room at the end of the corridor and we were in a 22 man room, not next door, but one or two doors down.

The barracks probably had about 14 rooms; there were seven or eight on each side. Each of those had the minimum of twenty people.

So the first day that we got there, there was a lot of camaraderie about finding out who was there that you knew. There were two guys from my crew, Ben Berg, the pilot, and Larry—I can't think of Larry's last name. He came from Covington, Massachusetts. I've been in contact with him all this time, chiefly at Christmas time.

There was one other guy, one other officer that didn't show up. We didn't know what had happened to him. And there were none of the enlisted men in our crew who were there. However, we did bump into a few people from the 392nd Bomb Group that were on the same mission that we were on, who were picked up at more or less the same time that we were and were on the various transports that we were on, although we don't recall seeing them at that point.

Now the guys in the room we were assigned to, none of them came from my Bomb Group, but they were all crewmen from bombers. There were no fighters in there, but there was a great assortment of guys from different outfits and we kind of introduced ourselves to one another and sort of one took charge of various duties that we would have in the functioning of the room from day to day.

We had one guy, his name was Ziggie, he volunteered to be in charge of our food situation. We really didn't know what the food situation was going to be, except that it was explained to us that we would be getting rations. The rations consisted of, as I recall, one loaf of black bread every day for six people. So it depended on how thin you could slice the bread to see how many slices each of you might get out of that loaf.

The other food that was given to us mostly on a daily basis were rutabagas, which is a big purple vegetable that I hadn't seen before, perhaps the size of a small watermelon, a musk melon. It was sort of a turnip like vegetable.

Then there were always a lot of potatoes and greens.

We never did get meat to speak of. Once in a while we got some horse meat ration, but whatever we got from day to day, was picked up by the people who were in charge of the food for each room—in our case, I don't remember who was in charge of getting the food, but it was all delivered to Ziggie, and Ziggie would do the apportioning and whatever cooking was done—there wasn't a heck of a lot of cooking, but there was some mashing of the potatoes and with the rutabagas. They were cut up and divided and after a while, everybody got pretty much organized as to what we were doing with the food that we were receiving from the Germans.

Now this was not enough to keep us alive, so it was supplemented by the Red Cross Parcels. The Red Cross was wonderful. In retrospect, now, I think that when we were in Wetzlar, the Red Cross gave us a cardboard box that had something like a sweater in it, a pair of gloves, a few little other items—a hat, a warm hat for your head, and a few little other items. The box was a handy box. It was a cardboard box, but we all had one and we kept our things in that in our room to separate our things from the rest of the other people's material possessions.

As you can imagine, with twenty guys in a relatively small room made up of triple decker beds, which were mattresses and slats—just boards, actually, across a frame, with straw being put into some sort of a net material, sort of like sacks the potatoes would come in or something like that. That was the mattress.

Anyway, to get back to the food situation, we did get a Red Cross Parcel, perhaps every two weeks. They were wonderful. They had a can which was called Klim, which is milk spelled backwards. This was a fairly large can of powdered milk which was very good to have around. We could do a lot of things with it. Ziggie could make things. We would contribute our various things to the community dining table for whatever he was going to prepare for us on any given day.

In addition to that, we had a couple of packages of cigarettes, what was called a D bar. This was a highly enriched chocolate bar, which was quite in vogue. Everybody was dealing in D bars. They used them for gambling or for betting with or things of that nature.

As an aside, I'll tell you that later, we used them for trading with the Germans for things that we wanted, because they didn't have any chocolate and they would love to get some chocolate and American cigarettes were very popular with them.

In addition, there were vitamins in that package, there was fish, either tuna fish or sardines, and sometimes some canned corned beef. Just thinking about it brings back such wonderful memories of our seeing this wonderful food when we opened up the can. It was a big day when we got our rations from the Red Cross.

They probably also sent us some clothing and stuff, but they didn't give us any of that. And I'll tell you about that later on.

That's sort of a summary of our general food situation. We got certain rations on a daily basis from the Germans, which we would administer ourselves, and we would supplement this with stuff we got from the Red Cross on a communal basis, and then other stuff we would keep privately for our own personal use.

In addition, some of the lucky guys who were there longer than we were, were getting regular food parcels from their loved ones at home and that was a big deal.

I personally never got any in the ten months I was in the prison camp, but some of the people did and some of them got letters as well, although I wasn't one of the fortunate ones in that regard.

After we got settled in the room and had our day to day situation, we were made aware of the organization in the camp.

The camp commander was General Zemke (Zemke was a Colonel. MC) a hot shot P-47 pilot who got shot down. He was a wheel, and he had all the rest of the wheels in his barracks where he was. So all of the Lt. Colonels and Majors, of which there was a fair sprinkling of them. I can remember Colonel Gabreski was there, Mozart Kaufman, he was a Major. He had 75 missions as a fighter pilot in a P-47 in Europe, and before that, he flew a P-40 in the Aleutian Islands and said they had more losses from weather in the Aleutians in those P-40 than he from the Japanese.

After he had done a tour there, he was sent back and checked out on P-47s, and sent to the ETO, and he just loved that P-47. He flew 75 missions. He could have gone home, but he liked that, he liked that more than anything he'd ever done in his life, so he just kept flying and doing that sort of stuff.

We also had a Colonel Spicer there. He was a West Point guy with a big walrus mustache. He was a spit and polish guys and always was giving the Germans a hard time. He'd lay down the law to all of us that we were not supposed to fraternize with the Germans and we were not supposed to talk to them except in an official manner and we certainly were not supposed to buddy up with them at all. And that was the way he wanted it to be.

He always was giving the Germans a hard time when we had Appell—that was roll call. We had roll call every morning about 6:30 or 7:00 o'clock when they'd count you all. Then they'd count you in the afternoon and in the evening again. They were always counting you.

This was sort of an official type of thing. The German high command was out there for every roll call to make sure to make sure they got the right numbers. There was a formality to go through, but it gave Col. Spicer a place to lecture to the troops. And he was not bashful about telling the POWs not to be nice to the Germans, because they were our enemies and we were fighting them and we weren't to have anything to do with them. We weren't to be abusive, but we were always calling the Germans goons. I don't know where that name came from, but the Germans were goons to us.

The Germans were a little bit baffled by the word goons. They wanted to know, "What does this mean?" We looked it up in the dictionary and we couldn't find it. We never did tell them what goons meant.

What I'm covering in this area is the orderly arrangement of chain of command. We, as American soldiers, took orders from the Camp Commander, that is the POW Camp Commander, and his echelon. He had an intelligence officer, a "this officer" and a "that officer", who was in charge of various things.

I was not privy to what was going on, but I imagine that they had an escape committee that was always working on plans for escaping. And then they also sort of controlled what activities we were doing in the camp in relationship to educational programs which we were developing for one another, or the library activities, which were going on. And whatever else that was being done in the prison camp that had to be organized by the POWs themselves.

There was someone in each barracks who was designated as the barracks leader. In our case, it was W. P. Jones and Dusty Rhodes. They would get orders from both the American Commanders and the German Commanders as to what their duties were in terms of this barracks.

We had to be out there for roll call at the proper time, discipline was to be maintained—no one was supposed to light the fires inside the rooms, the lights had to be out at the proper time, not molest the dogs that were in the prison camp after lights out was in effect.

Anyhow, those were the duties that had to be performed in each barrack building by the people who were in charge of that activity.

Periodically, we had to evacuate the barracks on short notice if the Germans decided they wanted to search the barracks for any contraband or whatever. They were always kind of picky about things that we might be doing that they might consider insulting to the Germans—any pictures you might be hanging up which were lampooning the German commander and what have you. They were always looking around for any contraband that we might have.

We used to make liquor—whiskey out of raisins and stuff. Some of the guys who distilled that material into some sort of an alcoholic brew. They didn't tolerate that if they found that. They would pick it up and spill it out. They didn't like it if people were keeping notebooks that were lampooning them in any way. If they came in and searched the barracks and anybody had any books lying around, they would thumb through it. If they found things they didn't like, they would confiscate them. They were kind of picky about that sort of thing.

After we were oriented as to what was going on, in general, in the camp, we found out that number 1, there was some library facilities. I think that the main library was over in the South Compound, which was an old compound. This had been a Prisoner of War Camp since 1939, when some of the British flyers had been shot down in the opening salvos of the war in September of '39 and were prisoners there.

We also had a British doctor and they had some clergymen over there. I never, personally, got into the South Compound, but that was a big established Compound. They had an auditorium and they had all sorts of nice things there, one of which was the library.

We were entitled to get books from that—I don't remember exactly how they were periodically delivered to our camp, but we did get a good smattering of 19th Century British authors like George Elliott, Oscar Wilde, and of course, we had Shakespeare books, but everything was kind of British. The books were pretty good, actually, and they were well read. That was one of the things that was pretty important.

And then they had a schedule of people who would give lectures, people who had talent to give lectures on literature or on history or on physics or whatever. There was a lot of talent in the Prison Camp and things would be organized in such a fashion so you could attend Italian lectures if you wanted to or French.

And we did have a sprinkling of people in the Prison Camp that were not Americans. We had a half a dozen or so French POWs, probably flying with the British, we had some Polish, and I think there were a couple of Italian nationals as well. In addition, there were a few Russians in the Prison Camp, but they were the ones assigned to do all the nasty jobs like emptying the Honey Buckets, which were the night soil in the latrines. Periodically they came along and collected all of the duty of the previous three or four days into buckets and they used it for fertilizer.

But we didn't have to do that. None of the officers had any work to do, so they had to find things to keep them amused. So the reading and the lectures were one thing.

There was a certain amount of ball playing. We didn't really have a soccer field, per se, but we used to kick around the soccer ball. There were some baseballs being thrown around and touch football was being played by certain groups. I don't recall participating in that, but I did know that it was going on.

They had a Glee Club that used to give sing-songs periodically.

You must remember that in the North Two Compound that we were in, there were probably twelve buildings there, twelve barracks. We were in Barracks number 9 that went up to, probably, Barracks number 12, and there were probably, in each barracks—like I said—fourteen rooms with about an average of 20 people in each room. So there were two hundred or more people in each barracks and multiply that by fourteen barracks, so there were more than 2,000 POWs in just North 2 Compound. It was probably opened in July or August of 1944 and was probably filled up by October or November, so they had to start building North Three Compound, which never got completely full, because by the time they opened up a few barracks in North Three Compound, it was pretty much in December of 1944 and things were winding down.

I have to tell you something about the toilet arrangements in the Camp. We had one large latrine which had urinals in the center section on either side, so perhaps thirty or forty people could be relieving themselves at any one time. And on the side there were biffies where you could sit down. They were not sheltered in any way and there were probably around thirty on either side, so that's 60 guys could be accommodated at one time, although I don't ever remember seeing more than fifteen or twenty at any one time in there.

The trader

As I indicated to you, it wasn't a very pleasant place to be and the Russians used to empty those Honey Buckets every three days, so it wasn't the type of a place that you wanted to congregate. We did use little portions of that for some of our surreptitious activities, which I will tell you about a little bit later, in terms of the trading that went on between the Germans and some of the designated people who were called "traders." Not traitors.

I guess this is as good a time to talk about the traders. After we were there for a month or so, the wheels somehow or other, found out that I could speak a little German. I was the only one in the barracks that could, so they had me come over one day and told me that I was going to be a trader.

"What does that guy do?"

Well, we periodically needed to get things from the Germans that we couldn't get in any other way. They evidently had a radio that needed a battery from time to time, so we had to get a battery from the Germans. That's the only thing that I ever got for them, although we did some petty trading for eggs and cigarettes and things of that nature, but every now and again, when they needed something, they would get the traders together and they would tell them what they needed and how we should go about it. They didn't want the Germans to know what we were trying to get things for.

One of my duties was to trade with the Germans, so I was one of those designated to be able to speak with them. So I got to know a number of them by name.

One of them was a guy by the name of Lammerick, who was kind of a rigid person. He was a strict interpreter of the rules and regulations and wasn't a very pleasant fellow. He did speak fairly good English, however, and in his official capacity, he did things in a typical Germanic fashion—by the numbers and it was always very correct, but not very pleasant.

But my duties as a trader, as I indicated, were fairly minimal in so far as the only thing I ever procured during the time I was there that was of any importance was a battery, and we had to be pretty surreptitious as to why we wanted a battery, etc. And of course, the German guards, we had to get to be very "in" with them by giving them chocolate or cigarettes or something over a period of time before we would slip it to them that we needed something and they had to come through for us as we had been friends with them.

I remember one of them asking me one day, "What is it this goon business?" They didn't like the fact that we were calling them goons and sort of laughing about it. He said he looked it up in the dictionary and couldn't find it.

So I told him that goons just meant a good friend, a good fellow.

Life goes on

I've telescoped a lot as ideas have come into my head.

After we had been there for a month or so, we began to get acclimated to the situation. You had made new friends, you had old friends there. The one thing that went on in the Prison Camp all the time was conversation. The conversation was about many, many things. Primarily it was about how little food we were getting and wouldn't it be nice if we could get a nice hamburger and French fried potatoes or something of that nature.

But I noticed that when the Red Cross parcels came, usually people had a pretty good meal that night and they were probably talking about girls, maybe their wives or sweethearts or how they missed them, etc. We never did see any women around that prison camp, because there were no German girls, either, to be seen either working there or any place around the prison camp.

But we did have personal conversations about many items in so-called Bull sessions. You certainly got a fractionation of population—all of the Southerners were fighting the Civil War all over again, the Texans were something special because they thought the whole war depended upon them, the people from Harvard always gave us a hard time about how smart they were. And they were. They were contributing to the activities of the camp.

But when asked, "What did you do all the time that you were there?" Well, conversation was a big item. I imagine there were people who were organizing escapes, but there never were any escapes from Stalag Luft I. Number one, if you got out of the camp, there was hardly any place to go. The Baltic Sea was just north of you and you couldn't get a row boat to go to Denmark in. And it was swampy, too.

If you went south or east or west, if you didn't speak German, you stood out like a sore thumb and you couldn't go very far before you got caught. It was kind of a losing battle.

We understood that in previous years, a few British did escape, but they were people who spoke fluent German and were sort of people who were designated to do things outside the camp and took advantage of their position to disappear and sneak aboard a Swedish vessel in Straalsand or something of that nature. But escape is not an option as far as we were concerned. I don't think there was any tunnel digging or anything that was going on in Stalag Luft I the way there was in Stalag III.

We did, of course, have a radio or two, but that was all pretty secret. But we were getting BBC every night. Somebody would write out the salient headlines and they were distributed in some surreptitious fashion so each barracks got it.

At nighttime, when the lights were out, this was passed around or whispered around how the war was coming and where the lines were drawn. And of course, this got to be pretty exciting after October-November of 1944 as the Allies were doing very well. And then the Russians were also doing very well and coming westward. People were yelling every night, "Where is Uncle Joe?"

And of course, the Germans took a dim view of that. We got word from the German commander that they didn't want to hear any more of this talk about Uncle Joe. Colonel Spicer told them to go to hell that they would do whatever they wanted to. They put poor old Colonel Spicer in the cooler—this was where they had isolation. He was in there a long time. They threatened him with court martial and shooting and it didn't seem to bother Colonel Spicer very much. He'd be in the cooler for a while and then he would come out. He'd damn them once again and they'd put him back into the cooler.

But he seemed to get away with it all right. Everybody was kind of proud of him for the way he handled the Germans. Most of us ordinary guys didn't open our mouth too much, because we didn't want to get into any more trouble than we were already in at that time.

We also had maps. I don't remember who made the maps, but periodically, we would get a map that was supposed to have been an escape map. It had pictures of a local road situation in and out of the Barth area as far as going to Rostock, which was on the Baltic Sea and to the west there was Stralsund or Stettin, which was to the east. They were fairly well drawn maps. I don't know what we were supposed to do with them, but they also had maps of the Elbe River in the West and the Oder River in the East and the military action that was going on with the Allies moving from the west to east and the Russians moving from the east to west and the Germans getting squeezed in between.

Up north where we were, there wasn't a great deal of military activity and there wasn't any place to move the POWs out of as they were moving them from the southern POW camps and the eastern POW camps. For some reason or other, the Germans seemed to want to hold on to the POWs, whether for political trading purposes or what have you.

There was also some question of what would happen to the American POWs if the Russians liberated the camp and all of the American Prisoners were under the control of the Russian Commander. Evidently that was something that did eventually happen and how it was resolved at the higher levels I'm not sure, but they kept the POWs in Stalag I there for quite some time, perhaps from the 1st of May until the 15th or 20th of May, until they were all evacuated by the Americans.

There was a rumor going around, like everything else, there were a lot of rumors going around, that if the Russians liberated the Prison Camp that we wouldn't be sent back to the American lines to the West, but they would take us into Russia and send us back to the Black Sea and Turkey or places like that. Sort of use the POWs as a political pawn in some way. But whether that was true or whether that was rumor, we had no way of knowing at that particular point.

Along about November the number of Prisoners coming in began to trickle off somewhat, but we were very anxious whenever they came in to do to them what was done to us. We would milk them for military information as to what was going on in the outside world, not only from a military standpoint, but from a social standpoint of the movies, football or baseball, or whatever took the interest of the American population there.

This business gave us all great hopes that things were moving towards the end, and that particularly happened in December when things looked very, very good and everybody was planning to evacuate the camp by Christmas time. As a matter of fact, someone had made a bet with someone else that we would be out of the Prison Camp by Christmas Day and that if we weren't out, he would kiss someone else's ass in front of everybody at Appell one morning.

Well, we were still there that morning, so sure enough at Appell, he pulled down his britches and the other one kissed him right in the place that he said he would. And that, of course, was an area for great laughter and consternation to the Germans, as you can imagine, that the Americans thought of it as a big joke and enjoyed it all.

However, things took a rather bad turn at the end of December. As the Battle of the Bulge started, probably in the middle of December, and gave the Germans a pretty good shot in the arm because things were going pretty good with them for a while. But things became very bad for us, particularly as their campaign faltered. Number one, Hitler had ordered that all of us be shot. I don't know who was going to shoot us. By that time, most of the guards had probably served with Bismarck in the war of 1870—they were old men of the Home Guard. Anybody that was young enough to carry a machine gun was out fighting the Russians. The rest of the guards were old geezers. Plus the Americans had sent a lot of literature through the air—leaflets and pamphlets that told people that if the person is at war and the American and Allied Prisoners were mistreated, that all of the population would be held responsible and be equally mistreated.

So nothing much came of that. But what eventually happened was bad. That is to say that the Red Cross Parcels abruptly stopped. We were advised that they didn't have any more and because of the war situation, they weren't getting through. This sounded plausible, but it was a big lie, because after the Germans evacuated the area in the beginning of May of 1945, we ransacked their supply places and they had tons and tons of Red Cross Food all in the boxes. They didn't steal them themselves. You've got to give them credit for that, but they sure didn't give them to us. And they were laying there for three or four months. That sort of made us pretty angry with them, that we didn't get it, but we were also pretty impressed with them that they didn't steal them themselves.

The other thing that was there, there were a lot of military overcoats and jackets and shoes. We never got any of that stuff the whole time we were there, even though they had a whole warehouse full of it. So it didn't endear them to us any more than they were endeared to us before that, I might say.

In any event, the events from January 1, 1945, were a mixed bag.

On the one hand, we were very happy with the news that the Russians were moving very rapidly towards the West and the Germans were being beaten down and the Russians were moving very fast in that (our) area. And also, the Americans, probably by February or so, had reached the Elbe River, which was only about 100 or 120 miles from where we were—as the crow flies anyhow.

The Germans, at this time, were trying to get the Americans to join with them against the Russians, but of course that was out of the question. Eisenhower probably made the decision that the Americans would not capture Berlin, but we didn't know that at this time, but would leave that honor to the Russians. And the Russians were moving as fast as they could; we were urging them on as we were yelling every night, "Come on Joe, come on Joe."

The German Commander took great umbrage about that and issued orders that we were not to be yelling for Joe to come or we would be shot. Of course, that didn't attenuate the yelling too much—it did a little bit, but there were still cries of, "Uncle Joe, where are you?" and that sort of business.

But things were winding down and everybody had the feeling that the end was near, especially as March of 1945 came about. And then, of course, we got the bad news in April that President Roosevelt had died. That created a big pall over the Prison Camp and great elation on the German side. They felt that now that our leader was dead, the war situation would change and the Germans would be in a position to win the war instead of losing it as they had been.

And of course, with the Allied Armies pressing them both East and West, it wasn't very rational to think about that, anyhow.

Taking pictures

Well, here we are at the middle of April. It looked as though the thing is going to be wound down pretty quickly. The whole mood and atmosphere in the Prison Camp was one of impatience and elation and enthusiasm. We could feel that the time was coming close when the war was going to be over.

April 30, the rumors were running wild that Hitler was dead, that the Russians were entering Berlin and the war was physically over. We were not certain of all of this at the moment, but by the time we, in Stalag Luft I, awakened on May 1, 1945, we realized that for us the war was over. Why?

The guard towers were empty. There were no German guards around. Everybody had disappeared.

We got the word from Colonel Zemke that last night the German military leaders were indicating that they were abandoning Stalag Luft 1 and turning over control to Colonel Zemke.

Colonel Zemke put his own people in charge, not so much of the guard towers but in each of the compounds, with strict orders that nobody was to be leaving the camp and order was to be maintained.

As far as I was, personally, concerned, as soon as I had word that there were no Germans left in the area, I disappeared out of Stalag Luft 1, out of the North 2 Compound, on the road to Barth, which was only about a mile and a half away, and obtained three cameras, packages of film, a number of other items of contraband, and rapidly returned to Stalag Luft 1, and began taking pictures of all of the camp sites and as many of the individuals as I could get together.

This was particularly true of Kriegsgefangen Barracks, number 209, where I had been billeted for the previous ten months. We took individual pictures, we took group pictures, we took pictures inside of the rooms in order to demonstrate where we used to eat our meals and how we used to eat them. We took pictures of everything we could think of, from the wheels of the Stalag 1 Administration down to as many of the lowest individuals, including some of the Russian slave laborers who were working, still, in the camp and had not yet escaped.

In addition, we had also ransacked the Flak School, which was less than a quarter of a mile away from the camp and found many winter uniforms there, long white coats and hats, which were great souvenirs for everybody, so as many of them as could be carried away were taken into the North 2 Compound, donned as souvenirs of war and pictures were taken of all of these people in those particular garbs.

People were also getting all sorts of souvenirs. The lucky ones were able to get some swords or Nazi helmets and things of that sort that the Americans were anxious to take home.

The Flak School was a well apportioned place with many interesting facilities present and, of course a lot of artifacts, which we collected in great numbers.

We also noted that there was also a slave labor camp in the vicinity in which the people had been mistreated and many ugly sights were noticed at that time as well. I don't remember seeing any people at the slave labor camp. We were just interested in seeing the material they had there and to gather up whatever we could as souvenirs. I have no further recollection.

When we got back into the camp that day, Colonel Zemke had made strict ruling that anybody who left the camp was to be Court Martialed as soon as possible and would be severely disciplined. In the meantime, he was keeping as much law and order as was feasible, although it was very difficult for him to keep everybody locked up for very long.

May 2 came around and May 3 came around. On the afternoon of May 3, something happened that was remarkable.

The Russians

A few Russians came into the camp. One of them was riding a horse. He was a Russian Colonel, presumably, and he was stinking drunk from Vodka. He had a .50 cal pistol in his hand and was shouting in Russian, which was translated by our Kriege buddy, Walter Brotchuk, that he wanted to know whether the Russians under his command had liberated this camp and were we not pleased to be free after being prisoners for so long, and if so, why we hadn't been breaking up the windows, burning the barracks, going into town and raping the women, and doing everything that good soldiers are supposed to do.

Colonel Zemke was, evidently, a little bit frightened at this drunken Russian Colonel brandishing a .50 cal. Pistol at his head, so he said to the boys, "OK, fellows, break up the joint a little bit, but don't ruin it, because we're going to have to be here for a while."

So you can imagine what that did to this pent up energy. So they began to break out windows and tear up the joint as much as they could, not realizing they were going to have to be there for another few days at least, until the Allies could make arrangements for them to be evacuated.

Subsequently, some of the Texas boys, not to be outdone, were able to round up a couple of cows and butchered one of them so that they were making steaks on a spit for the evening meal.

At the same time, people were running rampant around the prison camp, not knowing what to do with themselves after the Colonel had told them to break up the joint a little bit. They were sorry after a few days, because the place kind of calmed down and when the wind was blowing at night through the broken windows, you could see that they had done the wrong thing.

Nonetheless, on about 4 May, large numbers of Russians came to the camp. They were not fighting military people, but ancillary personnel around the periphery of fighting forces who were providing medical supplies and medical equipment and information about troops.

There was one guy, who was what they call a translator, who spoke five or six different languages; English was not one of them. However, I was able to converse with him a little bit in my broken German and Russian. He told me that there was no big fighting in this area, but they were going to try to keep as much peace in the area as possible until they could determine how we were to be repatriated to the American forces.

I had no idea at that point as to what was going on politically, but obviously, the Americans were negotiating with the Russians for permission to come and take the Prisoners of War out themselves.

Leaving the camp

I was a little bit impatient, so I asked the Russian translator, whose name was Ephraim Hanowitz and from whom I have a written message in German, to the effect that he was going to bring me a car that I requested the next day. We were going to try to get out on our own.

He was as good as his word. The next day he did bring a car for me and two pillowcases, one of which had five or six or eight pistols in it and the other had a bunch of cameras and some film. He told me I could trade with these, that money was no good, nobody wanted any money, they just wanted artifacts. He gave me a map and told me that the British lines on the Elbe River were only about 100 miles away.

So the next morning, I think it was Mr. Boychuk and I took off. He spoke a little bit of Russian and I spoke a little bit of German, and Mr. Hanowitz gave me a Russian Pass, written in Russian, saying that I was an American from the Barth Prison Camp and that I was OK and I was to be given whatever help necessary. I still have that pass in my scrapbook that I cherish.

We started out and made about 60 miles before we ran out of petrol. At that point, we went by foot for a while. By this time, it was getting to be dark. We found a German lady who had two young daughters who was afraid the Russians were going to come and rape them all, so she was glad to see us. We spent the night in that house.

The next morning, I think it was the 6th or the 7th of May, we made our way by various and sundry means, part of which was on horseback, but not for very long, and part of it was on a bicycle. One of us was walking and carrying the two bundles we had.

Paris, France

When we got to the British lines on the Elbe—they were actually on the East side of the Elbe River. We told them we were escaped Prisoners of War from Stalag Luft 1 and we had important information that had to go to the same section headquarters in Paris, so they were very obliging and got us an airplane lift to Paris.

When we got there, after much to do, I was able to find an old college friend of mine, whose name was William Rifkin, who was a Major in the Medical Administrative Corps. Bill Rifkin was one of these dynamic, Sammy run fellows, who was able to join the Army as a Buck Private in the Military Corps and within three years had risen to the rank of Major in Military Medical Administration and was, at this time, in charge of all civilian medical supplies for the whole ETU.

Bill spoke pretty fluent French, had a very spacious office, and was very, very nice to me.

The first thing he did was to take me to the PX and get me a clean uniform. I'd been wearing the one I'd had on since I was captured ten months before. He also got me some shoes and some other particulars necessary to look like a clean, young American officer. In addition, he sent a wire home to my family that I was OK and would be coming home shortly and took me down to the Hotel Poissonier and introduced me to the concierge and instructed him that he was to translate these pistols and cameras, as necessary, into Francs, because I was going to be a guest there for a few weeks.

Needless to say, I was utterly delighted with the situation. The next day, Bill and his friends invited me to the Longchamps Race Course, where he had a box and they were having a racing meet that day. We have some pictures from that outing, and I hope they are available to you as well, because they featured not only Bill Rifkin, who later on became a protégé, potitically, of Adlai Stevenson and was appointed as the American Ambassador to Luxembourg at some time, which he enjoyed very much. Later on in his military career, under the Kennedy Administration, he was again appointed as American Ambassador to Senegal and to the other city, but the capital is Conicree. It's adjacent to Senegal and was a French speaking country.

Unfortunately, poor Bill died before he was 50 years old from a massive heart attack. I particularly mourned him very much, because he was so very good to me. As a matter of fact, after I left him at Long Champs, I went back to my own devices and met up with Boychuk and we caroused around town for a few days and I became ill. I imagine I had bronchitis or the flu or something, so I called up Bill and told him that I was sick, what should I do.

He said I should take the Underground to a certain station and get off. There was a Military Facility there and I was to report to the Officer of the Day and told I was a casual officer in Paris on detached duty and was sick. I did that.

They admitted me and put me to bed and administered to me and took a Medical History, they got all the information that's now in my Military Form, copies of which I still have.

I was there for about ten days and recovered from my illness, so they discharged me back to the street and I went back to my hotel where my things were still there and everything was in good shape.

By that time, I thought I had had it with the situation as it was going on. I'd lost Boychuk during the ten days I was in the hospital, so I don't know what became of him. I did not see him again for ten years, where I bumped into him accidentally at a medical meeting in Chicago.

Going home

As far as my situation was concerned, I decided that I had better go home, so I reported to the Same Section Headquarters that I was an escaped Prisoner of War. I think this must have been about the 22nd or 23rd or 24th of May. They were all very enthusiastic and excited and said, "Fine, Lt., we're able to get you home by air if you want to. We have a plane leaving in a couple of days that we can probably get you on."

I thought to myself, "I'd probably better not push my luck any more. Who knows what the situation is with these airplanes and I'm in no particular rush. I want to take it easy for a while."

So I told them I would go home by ship if they didn't mind. They said they didn't mind at all, and they cut orders for me to go to Camp Lucky Strike, which was near Le Havre, where they evidently had a number of ships going out every three or four days, back to the States.

So that's what I did. I went to Camp Lucky Strike and checked in there. It wasn't a week—less than a week, probably, that I was assigned to the General Black, one of those small Liberty Ships. There were a lot of people waiting to get home at Camp Lucky Strike, so we got on board.

I had a footlocker this time, something like a footlocker or barracks bag—I can't remember exactly what, but I still had some cameras and some pistols that I'd gotten from Sergeant Hanowitz back in the Prison Camp, and wouldn't you know, they were stolen aboard ship on the way home. I wound up with one camera and one pistol that I happened to have on my person. Everything else was stolen from my footlocker underneath my bunk. As you can imagine, I was pretty damn mad. After all that time, to have all these looted by my own American compatriots—

However, nothing could be done about it. I just took it in stride. I laid around on the deck stripped down to the waist and got a little sun on the way home and took it as easy as I could until we reached Boston. That was our first Port of Call.

Unbeknownst to me, and because of the telegram Bill Rifkin had sent back to my folks, my older brother Nate found out which ship I was coming home on, and he was in Boston to meet me. He took me off the ship and back home with him. I didn't get orders for some time as to what to do, but when I finally got the orders, which I think came from the Military in Boston—I was all mixed up at that point and I don't know how things worked out, but I had orders to go on leave for 60 days and then to report to Atlantic City, New Jersey, sometime in late August or early September.

So, needless to say, we had a marvelous time with my family and all during that period. To wind this story up in typical fashion, I got back into a fairly normal situation, put on about thirty pounds of weight over all of this time, had to get some more new uniforms, and there I was in Atlantic City, feeling that I was going to be reassigned and probably put on another crew and sent back to war in the Pacific.

9/11, 1945

One morning, it was the 11th of September in 1945, when at breakfast, one of the guys said to me, "Hey, Jacobson, your name is on the Bulletin Board on a list of people who are eligible for immediate discharge."

I said, "Quit kiddin' me. I know I'm not gonna get discharged."

"Oh no, sure," he said, "it really is. Take a look."

And sure enough, I took a look and there was my name eligible for immediate discharge.

And that evening I was in Fort Dix, New Jersey, getting my shirts from the Air Force. I was just amazed. And here it was, the 11th of September 1945, exactly one year, to the day, that I was shot down in the vicinity of Hannover, Germany, on the 11th of September of 1944.

So there was a round about finality in the situation relative to that date, which was to me a milestone date in my life. Little did I know what was going to happen on the 11th of September in 2001.

Selected Pictures

*These pictures are From Coleman Jacobson's private collection,
And were taken by Coleman Jacobson, after the liberation of Camp,
1st and 2nd May, 1945*

by Erik Dyreborg

View of Camp. Picture taken from one of the towers.
The road to the left is the main road to Camp, and it's still there.
The forest to the left is also still there, but the area to the right now belongs to a farm. The Camp was burned down by the Russians shortly after the liberation, and there's practically nothing left, apart from a few barracks foundations, and pieces of concrete.

An ex POW, near the main road, where I(Erik Dyreborg) walked in May, 2004

A group of ex POWs in front of barracks 209

Afterword

By Erik Dyreborg

It was in the early spring of 2003, when I had my first talk with Lyle Shafer. A good friend, Margaret Cawood put me in touch with Lyle, when I was chasing WWII airmen stories for my next book, The Young Ones, which was published in June, 2003. Lyle told me that he was shot down over Germany in 1944 on his 25th mission on September 10, 1944, and that he was willing to let me have his story for my book. I later found out that the two other men in this book, were also shot down over Germany in September, 1944.

Lyle and I kept in touch, by phone and e-mail. In September, 2003 he told me about a reunion of ex POWs, which was going to take place in October, 2003. Furthermore, he told me, that they had their first reunion back in 1989. The reunion was made possible due to a list Lyle made while in prison camp in Germany during 1944 and 1945. Lyle also told me, that due to this list, he was able to track down all of his roommates in Stalag Luft I.

I understood that this wasn't just any POW story, so I asked Lyle his opinion about doing a book about him, his roommates, and how he found them all, after the war. Lyle immediately said that he was for it, and that he would discuss it with his former POW roommates during the reunion in October, 2003. It's not every day you get the opportunity to write a book about 25 men who were all in the air war over Europe in WWII, in the same POW camp, in the same barracks, No. 209, and even in the same room. At least I hadn't heard about a similar situation, until then.

After the reunion in October, 2003, Lyle got back to me, and had nothing but sad news. Most of the gathered ex POWs had no intention of contributing. Many of them gave Lyle the message that they were too old, that it was too long ago, and it had better be forgotten.

I was disappointed with the news, however, I understood and respected these men and their decision. But Lyle didn't give up. He started writing long letters to all of them explaining the importance of telling their stories about this unique team and their experiences during WWII.

Although most of them, did not respond to Lyle's letters he kept on chasing them. Lyle knew their stories and was very determined to have at least a couple of them for the book.

After some time, a few short stories started rolling in, but they were all much too short, could not be considered as a story, and merely facts.

Meanwhile, Lyle mailed me a lot of video tapes from the 55th anniversary reunion in 2000. I started watching those tapes, which gave me an opportunity to get acquainted with these men, i.e. in a very limited way. I watched the tapes, over and over again, but it was difficult, to get a complete story from them. Once again I contacted Lyle, asking him to locate one or two stories, and then write, partly his own story, and the story of how he tracked down all his roommates.

Through Lyle, I also got in touch with Steven Lian, who mailed me an unfinished manuscript from his father. I expected "the usual" 30-40 pages. However, one day the mailman dropped a 16 pound package on my doorstep. In the package, there were 4 volumes and about 1,000 pages written by Elmer T. Lian. I went through the 1,000 pages and had about a third of it typed off by a good friend, Sylvia Hill.

In May, 2004, Margaret Cawood and Sylvia Hill (sisters) came over to Denmark, and together, we made a one day trip to Stalag Luft I, Barth, Germany.

We met with Helga Radau over lunch who is very familiar with Stalag Luft I, and later she took us to the place where Stalag Luft I used to be. We saw everything there was to see. Besides the camp and the memorial, we went to the air field, where the liberated POWs were flown out. We went to the local school, where they have a huge model of the entire camp. We also went down to the train station, where all the POWs arrived, and were marched to the camp.

During our stay at the rail station, suddenly the local Police showed up, (mind you we were in old Eastern Germany), and asked us, why we were taking pictures of the rail station. I told them in my American-English, not in German, why we were there. However, they still found a bit odd that we were taking pictures of the rail station. I asked them why they were asking us these questions; and the older Officer told me, that someone called, and told them that some strange people were running around the rail station taking pictures. I told them that even Barth was now part of The West and that the STASI-days were over. That ended the conversation and they left.

The situation we experienced is a typical left over from the days when everyone in Eastern Germany should report anything abnormal. Oh yes, they still have it in them.

About a month later, Colemann Jacobson showed up with his wife. Since they were booked on a cruise out of Copenhagen, they visited one day; and I had Colemann's story recorded on tape. The tape was later transcribed by Maragaret Cawood and the result became Colemann's story; The 9/11.

Since Lyle and I now had the stories, we needed for the book, we decided to finish the book, together at his place in the States during one week in the summer of 2004, and I booked a flight and everything was arranged.

However, our regular day by day e-mail correspondence suddenly stopped—Lyle didn't reply to my e-mails. I kept sending reminders, and waited and waited; then one day, I decided to call. Fortunately it was answered by Lyle. He told me that he suddenly become very sick and had had to be flown by helicopter to a hospital in Seattle. There he would have to attend weekly check ups. From his voice, Lyle sounded weak, and we therefore decided that I should not fly over, at least not for awhile. So we cancelled the whole thing. We decided to finish the book, the best we could, by way of e-mail and phone calls; so we did.

Lyle and I worked on his own introduction and story, "Lyle's List", Elmer T. Lian's story, "The Experience", and Colemann's story, "The 9/11". We were done early 2005.

In the beginning of 2005, I had several talks with Lyle, and I could feel that he wasn't getting any better. Sometime in March, 2005, I had to call Steven Lian because I couldn't get in touch with Lyle by e-mail any more. Steven soon reported back, that Lyle had died on March 20th and was to be buried at Arlington, later in 2005.

I was indeed sad about Lyle's death. I'd lost a good friend. I was also sad because now Lyle would not be around when the book was published. He had been looking forward to it for a long time.

Lyle's death put a temporary stop to the book. My own situation even got worse financially. I lost my job when the American company I worked for, was taken over by another huge American operator, in spring 2005. When you're at my age, 60 years old, you're considered real old in Denmark, and no one wants to hire you. It's practically impossible to get a job.

However, due to donations from the Lian and the Shafer families, the necessary funds were raised, and the publication about these great men, and their remarkable story, has become a reality for which I'm truly grateful.

Last, but not least, I'd like to thank Steven Lian for all his kind help, and for his never quit and never give up attitude.

Erik Dyreborg
May, 2006

978-0-595-39781-5
0-595-39781-6

CPSIA information can be obtained at www.ICGtesting.com
Printed in the USA
LVOW06s2315101213

364799LV00002B/400/A